THOMAS MERTON

A BIBLIOGRAPHY

THOMAS MERTON

A BIBLIOGRAPHY

BY

FRANK DELL'ISOLA

FARRAR, STRAUS AND CUDAHY

NEW YORK

American Book-Stratford Press, Inc., New York

CONTENTS

INTRODUCTORY NOTE AND ADDENDA   vii

A. BOOKS AND PAMPHLETS BY THOMAS MERTON   1

B. BOOKS WITH CONTRIBUTIONS BY THOMAS MERTON   21

C. CONTRIBUTIONS BY THOMAS MERTON TO NEWSPAPERS
AND PERIODICALS   28

D. CRITICAL ARTICLES AND LETTERS ABOUT THOMAS
MERTON IN PERIODICALS, NEWSPAPERS AND BOOKS   39

E. TRANSLATIONS BY THOMAS MERTON   48

F. MISCELLANEA   53

G. THE POETRY OF THOMAS MERTON IN PERIODICALS,
NEWSPAPERS AND BOOKS   59

H. TRANSLATIONS INTO FOREIGN LANGUAGES OF BOOKS,
POEMS, AND ESSAYS BY THOMAS MERTON   69

I. THE UNPUBLISHED WORKS OF THOMAS MERTON   77

J. JUVENILIA   89

INDEXES   95

INTRODUCTORY NOTE

This bibliography is an expanded and revised version of an earlier work of mine, *A Bibliography of Thomas Merton,* which was published in *Thought.**

In compiling this initial bibliography of Thomas Merton, the descriptive method used in listing his American First Editions is similar to the form adopted by the American Library Association and used in the cards printed and distributed by the Library of Congress. I have taken certain liberties with the standard procedure of listing which wholly ignores blank leaves and unnumbered printed preliminary leaves, in order to account for all leaves, either those upon which any printing appears, or blanks, or end-papers, the better to establish the priority of a First Edition.

Only the American First Editions of Thomas Merton are described in detail, except the two English entries in section "F" which are bibliographically significant. Later editions and impressions are wholly ignored except those of bibliographical import.

The index pattern does not adhere to a unified alphabetical sequence. For ease and immediate reference it has been divided into nine separate sections, i.e.,

BOOK INDEX
INDEX OF MERTON ARTICLES
INDEX OF ARTICLES ABOUT MERTON
POETRY INDEX
INDEX OF FOREIGN PUBLICATIONS

---

* Fordham University Quarterly, XXIX, 115 (Winter, 1954–55), [574]-96.

Introductory Note

INDEX OF TRANSLATORS
INDEX OF UNPUBLISHED ITEMS, ETC.
INDEX OF JUVENILIA
INDEX OF NAMES

All books, pamphlets, newspapers, periodicals and records described and noted herein have been personally examined by me (except where indicated) and form a part of my library. Definitiveness has been my constant objective but a bibliography, however comprehensive it purports to be, can never be complete while the author is still engaged in writing.

Mention here should be made of two rare items of Merton's which were published in England in 1930, when he was fifteen. An essay entitled "Titus Oaks" was published in the Grantham *Journal* and another entitled "A Famous Old Oakhamian" was published in the Lincoln, Ruthland and Stamford *Mercury*. Correspondence to these newspapers has brought no response.

From Father Louis I have learned that parts of *Seeds of Contemplation* appeared in Polish behind the Iron Curtain and excerpts translated into Czech have been published in England; I has seen neither. Merton also wrote the text and prayers for two prayer-cards (one for the Feast of Saint Joachim, and the other for the centenary celebration of the founding of Gethsemani) which were published at Gethsemani (no longer available; I have not seen them). Finally, Father Louis was also responsible for a piece, "The Man of Great Possessions," which may have appeared in Friendship House *News* (1941 or 1942); I could not track this down. This magazine also reprinted a poem, "Holy Communion: The City," which I was unable to locate. There is also an article, "Il Papa Della Madonna," which Merton wrote for inclusion in a commemorative volume given to Pius XII on his 80th birthday, and published in Italy by the Pontifical Academy of Sciences; I have not seen it.

It was not deemed bibliographically significant to list and describe in detail the poetry work-sheets of published poems and other manuscripts which are housed in the libraries of the University of Buffalo, the University of Kentucky, Boston College, and Saint Bonaventure University (which has much unpublished material). But the major part of Thomas Merton's manuscripts, published and unpublished, are in the custody of Sister M. Thérèse Lentfoehr, of Saint Mary's Hospital, Wausau, Wisconsin.

I would like to extend to Mr. Richard Bourette, wherever he may be, my heart-felt thanks for first bringing the writings of Thomas Merton to my attention; to M. James Fox, O.C.S.O., Abbot of Our Lady of Gethsemani, for permission to visit and work in the Monastery library; to Thomas Merton for his invaluable suggestions and assistance and his infinite patience in answering my numerous queries and occasionally sending me a flow of items of which I would never have known; to Fr. Irenaeus Herscher, O.F.M., Librarian of Saint Bonaventure University, for graciously loaning me the rare, bound volume of *The Oakhamian* and dispatching from his library the bulk of Merton's foreign items; to Mr. Robert Giroux, editor-in-chief of Harcourt, Brace from 1948 to 1955 and now editor and vice-president of Farrar, Straus and Cudahy, whose counsel and encouragement made this bibliography possible; to Misses Naomi Burton and Jean Rosenthal, of Curtis Brown, Ltd., for their continued interest and help; and to Mr. Christy Dukas who helped immeasurably in the mechanics of the work.

Special thanks are due to the staffs of the following university libraries: Columbia, Fordham, and Saint John's (downtown and uptown branches in Brooklyn), for their response to my constant research demands; to the members of the New York Public Library, Reference Department, Room 315, for their patient help and guidance; to their Newspaper Annex for rendering invaluable aid and assistance; to Mr. James A. Wechsler, editor of the New York *Post,* for permission to work in the newspaper's library.

To the staff of the Central Branch of the Brooklyn Public Library, at Grand Army Plaza, I offer my deep acknowledgement for their efficient help and courteous service and cooperation at all times. Particular thanks are due to Mr. Marino J. Ruffier, Assistant Coordinator of Central Service, for his generous aid in calling errors and omissions to my attention and his kindness in proof-reading the final draft; and to Mr. Theodore Avery, Jr., for his patient help, advice and guidance.

For bringing to my attention omitted items, supplying foreign

Introductory Note

material and for other bibliographical help, I am thankful also to the late Abbé Robert Kothen, Father P. Leo Van Dijk, O.C.S.O., Annemarie Von Puttkamer, Baroness Elisabeth von Schmidt-Pauli, Mrs. Daniel Gaudin, Mme. Marie Tadié, Mr. Mariano Del Pozo, Father Agostino Gemelli, O.F.M., Father D. Costanzo Somigli, O.S.B., Mr. David Gibble, Sister M. Thérèse Lentfoehr, S.D.S., Messrs. John Brunini and Edward S. Skillin; and to Hollis and Carter, Ltd. of London.

And a final word of thanks and acknowledgement to my wife Mildred, for her diligent application in the laborious task of reading and correcting each draft; her interest in the work had never flagged.

F. D.

ADDENDA

At this writing I have received a German edition of "Vom Sinn Der Kontemplation," which is a translation (by Alfred Kuoni) of "What Is Contemplation?"; it was published in 1955 by Verlag Der Arche in Zurich.

From Buenos Aires (Editorial Sudamericana) comes the following information: "Los Hombres No Son Islas," is a translation, by Gonzalo Meneses Ocon, of "No Man Is An Island," and it is to appear in December (1956).

There is also a hitherto unpublished set of two conferences on the priestly life, "Il Sacerdote In Unione Con Maria Immacolata," which has been published in *Convivium*, a new Italian periodical brought out in Rome, Italy, by the Priests' Society for the Adoration of the Blessed Sacrament (1956—Anno 1—pp. 26-36).

Jubilee magazine, in its April 1956 issue (3. 12; pp. [6]–9), ran an excerpt from "The Living Bread" entitled, "The Second Coming."

"Blake, Hopkins and Thomas Merton," an article by Sister Mary Julian Baird, R.S.M., it appeared in *The Catholic World* (April 1956. 183. 1093; pp. [46]–9).

[x]

A

---◆---

BOOKS AND PAMPHLETS

BY

THOMAS MERTON

ARRANGED CHRONOLOGICALLY

A. *Books and Pamphlets*

A1.   THIRTY POEMS*   1944

First edition:

THIRTY/POEMS/THOMAS MERTON/NEW DIRECTIONS
/THE POETS OF THE YEAR/NORFOLK: CONNECTICUT

[30] pp., 1 blank leaf. 22 x 16 cm. $1.00. Tan paper boards
lettered in maroon on front cover. Tan dust-wrapper printed
in maroon on front cover.

Also in paper edition. [30] pp., 1 blank leaf. 22½ x 15 cm.
50¢. Tan dust-wrapper printed in maroon on front cover.
Similar format as bound issue.

Colophon (p. [29]): Designed for New Directions by Algot
Ringstrom/and printed at The Marchbanks Press, New York
City, in July, 1944/The Types used are Kenntonian and
Lombardic initials
[Published: Nov. 20, 1944.]

A2. A MAN IN THE DIVIDED SEA 1946

First edition:

A/MAN/IN/THE/DIVIDED/SEA/by/THOMAS/MERTON

Title-page enclosed in design consisting of three closely
spaced rectangles forming a border. On verso of title-page:
COPYRIGHT 1946 BY NEW DIRECTIONS/NEW DIREC-
TIONS, 500 FIFTH AVE., New York City 18

155 pp., 1 leaf, 1 blank leaf. 23½ x 15½ cm. $2.50. Black
cloth lettered downward in gold on spine. Oyster-white dust-
wrapper, black border, printed in black and white on front
cover and downward on spine in white.

Colophon (p. [157]): A/MAN IN/THE DIVIDED SEA/
WAS PRINTED AT THE/PRESS OF DUDLEY KIMBALL.

---

* The dedication on verso of page [1] which reads: "Virgini Mariae, Reginae
Poetarum/Sanctissimae Dei Genitrici Ac Semper" should read: "Reginae
Poetarum, Sanctissimae Dei Genitrici/Ac Semper Virgini Mariae"; without
Merton's knowledge the last two words were moved to the beginning of the
dedication.

A. Books and Pamphlets

/The type-face used throughout/is Electra. ROBERT
LOWRY/designed the jacket/and the title/page/V
[Published: Aug. 25, 1946.]

CONTENTS: Author's Note—Song—Poem: 1939—The Man
in the Wind—Ariadne—The Oracle—Tropics—Fugitive—
Ash Wednesday—Song—Some Bloody Mutiny—Crusoe—
Dirge—A Song—April—The Greek Women—Calypso's
Island—The Pride of the Dead—The Bombarded City—
The Storm at Night—The Ohio River: Louisville—The
Dreaming Trader—The House of Caiphas—Aubade: Har-
lem—Aubade: The Annunciation—Dirge for a Town in
France—Aubade: The City—The Peril—Advent—Carol—
How Long we Wait—A Letter to my Friends—The Candle-
mas Procession—Cana—The Widow of Nain—St. Paul—
Trappists, Working—The Snare—An Invocation to St.
Lucy—St. Thomas Aquinas—St. Alberic—The Image of
True Lovers' Death—The Fall of Night—The Biography
—The Betrayal—Rahab's House—After the Night Office:
Gethsemani—Song for the Blessed Sacrament—The Word:
A Responsory—The Dark Encounter—The Victory—The
Trappist Cemetery: Gethsemani—A Whitsun Canticle
(Envoi)—Ode to the Present Century—St. John Baptist—
Clairvaux—La Salette

This volume also contains all of the poems which were published in Thomas Merton's first book of poetry: Thirty Poems;
the contents follow (pp. 113-55):

Lent in a Year of War—The Flight into Egypt—Prophet—
The Dark Morning—Song for Our Lady of Cobre—The
Night Train—Saint Jason—The Messenger—The Regret—
Aubade: Lake Erie—Poem—For my Brother—Death—Iphi-
genia: Politics—The Winter's Night—The Communion—
Holy Communion: The City—The Vine—The Evening of
the Visitation—In Memory of the Spanish Poet—The
Trappist Abbey: Matins—Evening—The Blessed Virgin
Mary Compared to a Window—Dirge for the Proud World
—The Holy Sacrament of the Altar—Ariadne at the Laby-

[4]

rinth—An Argument: Of the Passion of Christ—St. Agnes:
A Responsory—The Holy Child's Song—The Sponge Full
of Vinegar

A3. GUIDE TO CISTERCIAN [1948] LIFE

First edition:

Guide/to/Cistercian Life/[by Thomas Merton]/[Latin cross im-
print]/Our Lady of Gethsemani/Trappist P.O., Kentucky
    15 pp. 13½ x 8½ cm. (No Price.) Light blue paper printed
in black (n.p., n.d.).

A4. CISTERCIAN 1948 CONTEMPLATIVES

First edition:

CISTERCIAN CONTEMPLATIVES/Monks of the Strict Ob-
servance at/OUR LADY OF GETHSEMANI, KENTUCKY/
OUR LADY OF THE HOLY GHOST, GEORGIA/OUR
LADY OF THE HOLY TRINITY, UTAH/[by Thomas Mer-
ton]/A Guide to Trappist Life
    62 pp. 23 x 15½ cm. $1.00. Blue-grey boards lettered in
maroon on front cover; blue-grey end-papers. No dust-wrapper.
25 black and white photographs.
    Also in paper edition. 62 pp. 24 x 16 cm. 75¢. Blue-grey
paper printed in maroon on front cover. Similar format as
bound issue.
    Colophon (p. [63]): This Guide is published by/The Monks
of Our Lady of Gethsemani/Trappist, Kentucky/A First Edition of 10,000 copies was printed/January MCMXLVIII/by
the/Marbridge Printing Company, Inc./New York

[5]

A5.   FIGURES FOR   1948
                 AN APOCALYPSE

First edition:

FIGURES/FOR AN/APOCALYPSE/by/THOMAS/MERTON

Title-page enclosed in design consisting of three closely spaced rectangles forming a border. On verso of title-page: COPYRIGHT 1947 BY NEW DIRECTIONS/NEW DIRECTIONS, 500 FIFTH AVENUE,/NEW YORK CITY 18

111 pp. 23½ x 15½ cm. $2.50. Black cloth lettered downward in gold on spine. Cream dust-wrapper, black border, printed in black and white on front cover and downward on spine in white.

Colophon (p. [112]): THIS BOOK WAS PRINTED BY/ DUDLEY KIMBALL AT HIS PRESS/IN PARSIPPANY, NEW JERSEY

[Published: Mar. 18, 1948.]

CONTENTS: Figures for an Apocalypse—(Advice to my Friends Robert Lax and Edward Rice, to get away while they still can.)—(Cf. Apoc. xiv, 14.)—Landscape, Prophet and Wild-Dog—In the Ruins of New York—Landscape: Beast—The Heavenly City—Landscape: Wheatfields—Two States of Prayer—A Letter to America—Three Postcards from the Monastery—On the Anniversary of my Baptism—Song: Contemplation—A Mysterious Song in the Spring of the Year—Canticle for the Blessed Virgin (Envoi)—Duns Scotus—Two Desert Fathers: St. Jerome, St. Paul the Hermit—Spring: Monastery Farm—St. John's Night—The Song of the Traveller—Evening: Zero Weather—The Transformation: For the Sacred Heart—Rievaulx: St. Ailred—Theory of Prayer—Clairvaux Prison—Natural History—A Christmas Card—Winter Afternoon—Freedom as Experience—The Sowing of Meanings—Pilgrims' Song—The Landfall—The Poet, to his Book

This volume also contains an essay: Poetry and the Contemplative Life (pp. 95-111) which was originally printed in The Commonweal (see C14).

A. Books and Pamphlets

A6. EXILE ENDS IN GLORY 1948

First edition:

Exile/Ends in Glory/The Life of A Trappistine/MOTHER M. BERCHMANS, O.C.S.O./by/Thomas Merton/THE BRUCE PUBLISHING COMPANY/MILWAUKEE

3 leaves, vii-xii, 1 leaf, 1-311 pp. 22 x 15 cm. $3.75. Grey cloth lettered in black on spine with design. Green dust-wrapper printed in white on front cover with crayon sketch of convent; printed in white on spine. Back cover: About the author . . ./THOMAS MERTON

Errata: back cover of dust-wrapper: par. 3, line 3: "Griswold" is spelled "Griswald"; par. 8, line 3: sentence reading: "His a talent for beyond" should read: "His [is] a talent [far] beyond"; subsequent editions do not have comments.

6 black and white photographs.

[Published: Je. 25, 1948.]

CONTENTS: The Convent of the Redemption—An Interval in Lyons—The Convent at Laval—The Novice—Sentence of Exile—The Journey—Another Orphanage—At Work in the House of God—The Chicken Coop—New Stability—A Vocation Within a Vocation—The Child of Mary—At the Gate—A Canticle of Gratitude—Mistress of the Novices—"Via Crucis"—"Via Crucis"—(continued)—Calvary—Epilogue

A7. THE SEVEN STOREY 1948 MOUNTAIN

a. First edition:

THOMAS MERTON/The Seven Storey/Mountain/[quotation in two lines]/Harcourt, Brace and Company : : New York

5 leaves, 3-429 pp., 1 blank leaf. 21 x 14 cm. $3.00. Off-white cloth lettered in black on spine. Grey dust-wrapper, red-tan spine, printed in black and red on front cover, black and white

A. Books and Pamphlets

on spine. On front cover, lower case, a rectangular framed in red with comments printed in black on a white background; on back cover: 3 photographs of Trappist life.
On verso of title-page: first edition
[Published: Oct. 4, 1948.]

> CONTENTS: (Part One)—Prisoner's Base—Our Lady of the Museums—The Harrowing of Hell—The Children in the Market Place—(Part Two)—With a Great Price—The Waters of Contradiction—(Part Three)—Magnetic North—True North—The Sleeping Volcano—The Sweet Savor of Liberty—(Epilogue)—Meditatio Pauperis in Solitudine—Index

b. Reprint edition:

THOMAS MERTON/The Seven Storey/Mountain/[quotation in two lines]/Garden City Books · Garden City, New York

> 1 blank leaf, 5 leaves, 3-429 pp., 4 blank leaves. 21½ x 14 cm. $1.98. Black cloth lettered in gold on spine. Light grey dustwrapper printed in black and red on front cover and spine.
> On verso of title-page: Garden City Books Reprint Edition 1951,/by special arrangement with Harcourt, Brace and Company
> [Published: Feb. 5, 1951.]

c. Paper-back edition:

The Seven Storey/Mountain/by/THOMAS MERTON/[quotation in two lines]/[publisher's symbol]/A SIGNET BOOK/Published by THE NEW AMERICAN LIBRARY

> 511 [1] pp. 18 x 11 cm. 50¢. Blue and green paper printed in black, white, yellow and green on front cover with pictorial scenes showing the gamut of Man's life, and downward on spine in black and white; edges stained yellow.
> On verso of title-page: First Printing, April [30,] 1952

[8]

A. Books and Pamphlets

A8. WHAT IS CONTEMPLATION 1948

First edition:

What Is Contemplation/by/Thomas Merton, O.C.R./[ornament]/Printed at/Saint Mary's College/Notre Dame/Holy Cross, Indiana/1948

25 pp., 1 blank leaf. 21½ x 15 cm. 50¢. Salmon paper printed in black on front cover [ornament].
[Published: Dec. 8, 1948.]

A9. SEEDS OF CONTEMPLATION 1949

a. First edition:

Seeds of Contemplation/by Thomas Merton/A NEW DIRECTIONS BOOK [device]

1 blank leaf, 13-201 pp., 2 blank leaves. 22 x 14½ cm. $3.00. Tan burlap cloth with pale green label pasted on front cover and spine lettered in darker green, downward on spine. Cream dust-wrapper, with design, printed in black on front cover and downward on spine.

Colophon (p. [202]): THIS BOOK WAS PRINTED BY PETER BEILENSON,/MOUNT VERNON, NEW YORK, IN THE WEISS AND/CASLON TYPES, ON A SPECIALLY-MADE PAPER./FEBRUARY MCMXLIX.
[Published: Mar. 2, 1949.]

CONTENTS: Author's Note—Seeds of Contemplation—Everything That is, is Holy—Things in Their Identity—Pray for Your Own Discovery—We Are One Man—A Body of Broken Bones—Solitude—The Moral Theology of the Devil—Integrity—The Root of War is Fear—Hell as Hatred—Faith—Tradition and Revolution—Through a Glass—Qui Non Est Mecum—Humility Against Despair—Freedom Under Obedience—What is Liberty—Detachment—Mental Prayer—Distractions—The Gift of Understanding—The Night of the Senses—The Wrong Flame—Renunciation—Inward Destitution—Contemplata Tradere—Pure Love

[9]

A. Books and Pamphlets

b. Signed edition:

1 leaf, 1 blank leaf, 13-201 pp., 2 blank leaves. 22 x 14½ cm. $7.50. (Similar publication date, format, binding, dust-wrapper as trade edition.) On recto of leaf 1: Of this edition, one hundred copies/have been signed by the author/[signed] Thomas Merton.

Top edges stained green; in brown slip-case.

c. Revised edition:

5 leaves, xi-xvi, 1-191 pp. 21½ x 13½ cm. $3.00. Off-white sack cloth with cream label pasted on front cover and spine lettered in green, downward on spine.

On verso of title-page: Seventh Printing/First Revised Edition [Published: Dec. 19, 1949.]

In this revised edition, besides "A Preface to the Revised Edition", Chapter 14 reads: "ELECTA UT SOL" which had originally read: "QUI NON EST MECUM". The latter becomes Chapter 15 and follows the original sequence of chapter headings.

d. Paper-back edition:

THOMAS/MERTON/SEEDS OF/CONTEMPLATION/ [Christian symbol]/A DELL BOOK

189 [1] pp., 1 leaf. 16 x 11 cm. 25¢. Blue paper printed in black, white and yellow on front cover and downward on spine in white; edges stained blue.

On verso of title-page: Published by the Dell Publishing Company, Inc./261 Fifth Avenue, New York 16, New York [Published: Sept. 22, 1953.]

This edition has Christian symbols at end of chapters which were drawn by Rudolf Koch; the table of contents has been omitted as well as the frontispiece reproduction of Our Lady of Fontenay (XIIth century; San Vageot *) which was in all the bound editions.

---

* A note from Thomas Merton indicates that "San Vageot" is a publisher's misprint for the name of the photographer; it should read: "Yvonne Sauvageot."

A. Books and Pamphlets

A10. GETHSEMANI MAGNIFICAT 1949

First edition:

GETHSEMANI/MAGNIFICAT/CENTENARY OF/GETH-
SEMANI ABBEY/[by Thomas Merton]/[ornament]/
MCMXLIX/TRAPPIST, KENTUCKY, U.S.A.

[72] pp. 30½ x 23 cm. $2.50. Dull blue, pebbled boards let-
tered in gold on front cover. A reproduction of a scene of
monks at prayer and the Blessed Mother standing before them
is pasted on front cover on a gold background within a double,
gold border; deep-rose end-papers. No dust-wrapper.

200 photographs.

Colophon (*p.* [71]): Designed, printed and lithographed in
U.S.A./by the Fetter Printing Company, Louisville, Ky.

[Published: Ap. 5, 1949.]

A11. THE WATERS OF SILOE 1949

a. First edition:

THE WATERS/OF SILOE/THOMAS MERTON/Harcourt,
Brace and Company New York

6 leaves, xi-xxxvii, 1 leaf, 3-377 pp. 21½ x 14½ cm. $3.50.
Light blue cloth with device imprinted in gold on front cover;
lettered in gold on spine; photographed end-papers by Yvonne
Sauvageot. Top edges stained blue. Green-blue dust-wrapper,
with design, printed in white and black on front cover and
spine.

36 photographs.

On verso of title-page: first edition

[Published: Sept. 5, 1949.]

> CONTENTS: (Part One)—Prologue—Note on the Function of
> a Contemplative Order—Monasticism; St. Benedict; the
> Cistercians—De Rance and La Trappe—The Dispersal;
> First Trappists in America—Foundations in Kentucky and
> Illinois—The Trappists in Nova Scotia; Petit Clairvaux—
> The Foundation of Gethsemani Abbey—Gethsemani in the

A. Books and Pamphlets

Nineteenth Century; Other American Foundations—Reunion of the Cistercian Congregations; New Growth; Gethsemani under Dom Edmond Obrecht—Eight American Foundations—A Contemplative Order in Two World Wars—The Rising Tide: New Foundations in Georgia, Utah, and New Mexico; the Last Mass at Yang Kia Ping—(Part Two)—Cistercian Life in the Twelfth Century—The Cistercian Character and Sanctity—Paradisus Claustralis—Bibliography—Glossary of some Monastic Terms—Index

b. Reprint edition:

THE WATERS/OF SILOE/THOMAS MERTON/Garden City Books · Garden City, N.Y.

6 leaves, xi-xxxviii, 1 leaf, 3-377 pp. 21 x 14 cm. $1.98. Alice-blue cloth with device imprinted in gold on front cover; lettered in gold on spine; photographed end-papers by Yvonne Sauvageot. Top edges stained green-blue. Green-blue dust-wrapper, with design, printed in white and black on front cover and spine.

36 photographs.

On verso of title-page: Garden City Books Reprint Edition 1951,/by special arrangement with Harcourt, Brace & Company [Published: Feb. 5, 1951.]

A number of disparities exist in "A Note on the Function of a Contemplative Order" in these two editions which bear mention. In the First Edition (p. xxxiv), line 18 reads:

"The best religious Order is the one which performs most faithfully and exactly its own particular function in the Church, sanctifying its members and saving souls in the precise way laid down for it in the designs of God and by the dispositions of the Holy See. This means that the best Orders are the ones which are able to cling most closely to the ideal of their founders and to live their lives most perfectly according to their own particular Rules."

The Reprint Edition version (p. xxxiv), line 18 reads:

"The best religious Order is the one that has the highest end and the most perfect means for arriving at that end. This, at least, is the abstract standard by which we judge the difference between Orders. But in the concrete, the Order which comes closest to keeping its own Rule perfectly and which, at any given moment, best achieves the end for which it was instituted, will be, in point of fact, the best one in the Church at that moment. And therefore one Order cannot improve itself by suddenly deciding to adopt the institutions and aims of some other Order which has an entirely different purpose in the Church. Instead of becoming better, such an Order would only decline because it would be trying to do a work for which it was never intended."

In the paragraph which deals with Father Garrigou-Lagrange and Father Joret (p. xxxv), line 5, the First Edition does not have a footnote to clarify a point; the Reprint's footnote for line 11 (p. xxxv) reads:

"We must say that the Apostolic life tends principally to contemplation which fructifies in the apostolate." (Garrigou-Lagrange, "The Three Ages of the Interior Life", St. Louis, 1948, Vol. 2, p. 492.) "The life of union with God marks the summit of the Dominican life, the apostolate finds its source there." (Joret, "The Dominican Life", p. 82.)

Finally, in the First Edition (p. xxxvi), line 5, paragraph ends with: ". . . and has too often proved to have been so." This is followed by a new paragraph (line 6) beginning: "A Trappist monastery," etc.; but in the Reprint version (p. xxxvi), line 14, the sentence which reads: ". . . has too often proved to have been so" is followed with these additional comments (same line):

"An even more obvious danger is the materialism into which monks who are also professionally farmers can sometimes fall when they attach more importance to the business of running their farm than to the contemplative life which is their real end. The necessity to maintain industries in order to support their monasteries has also proved to be a considerable hardship to the Trappists. Teaching school may be a work of the active life, but at least it is a highly spiritual activity compared with the brewing of beer, the manufacture of chocolate, and the large-scale marketing of cheese. It was perhaps excessive materialism which really ruined the Cistercian Order in its golden

[13]

age. The zeal for manual labor as an adjunct to the contemplative life turned into a zest for land-grabbing and business which utterly ruined the contemplative spirit and introduced avarice, and the confusion of much activity, where there should have been the calm recollection that is born of poverty of spirit."

This is then followed by a "new" paragraph (p. xxxvi), line 31, which reads: "A Trappist monastery," etc.

A12.   THE TEARS OF THE   1949
              BLIND LIONS

First edition:

THOMAS MERTON/THE TEARS/OF THE/BLIND LIONS/
NEW DIRECTIONS

32 pp. 21½ x 14 cm. $1.25. Light blue cloth lettered downward on spine in black. Pale blue dust-wrapper printed in brown on front cover and downward on spine.

Also in paper edition. 32 pp. 21 x 13½ cm. 50¢. Pale blue dust-wrapper printed in brown on front cover; supplied with a cream mailing envelope. Similar format as bound issue.

[Published: Nov. 15, 1949.]

A13.   WHAT ARE THESE   1950
              WOUNDS?

First edition:

WHAT ARE/THESE WOUNDS?/THE LIFE OF A CISTER-
CIAN MYSTIC/Saint Lutgarde of Aywieres/By THOMAS MER-
TON/THE BRUCE PUBLISHING COMPANY/MILWAUKEE

3 leaves, vii-xiv, 1-191 pp. 21½ x 14½ cm. $2.50. Grey cloth lettered in black on front cover and spine. Blue dust-wrapper, with picture of nun and imprint of stigmatic foot, printed in

A. Books and Pamphlets

white, pale blue and grey on front cover, white and grey on spine.

[Published: Feb. 28, 1950.]

> CONTENTS: Preface—Childhood. Student in the Benedictine Convent. Two Suitors. Her First Mystical Graces—Prioress at St. Catherine's—Aywieres. The Albigensians. Her First Seven Year Fast—The Souls in Purgatory. Her Power Over Demons. Her Power of Healing—Sinners—The Spirituality of St. Lutgarde. Her Mysticism—St. Lutgarde's School of Mysticism at Aywieres. Her Relations With the Order of Preachers—Last Years and Death of St. Lutgarde —After Her Death. Miracles. Cult—Bibliography

A 14. A BALANCED LIFE 1951 OF PRAYER

First edition:

A Balanced/Life of Prayer/[Ornament]/THOMAS MERTON, O.C.S.O.

[1]-22 pp., 1 leaf. 15 x 9 cm. 10¢. Cream paper printed in brown.

On verso of p. 21, lower case: This pamphlet is published by/The Cistercian Monks of the Strict Observance/(Trappists)/ Copyright 1951 by the Abbey of Gethsemani/Trappist, Kentucky

[Published: Jl. 30, 1951.]

A 15. THE ASCENT TO TRUTH 1951

First edition:

THE/ASCENT/TO/TRUTH/[device]/Thomas Merton/[quotation in five lines]/Harcourt, Brace and Company, New York

3 leaves, vii-x, 1 leaf, [3]-342 pp. 22 x 15 cm. $3.50. Black cloth with device imprinted in gold on front cover; lettered in

gold on spine; photographed end-papers by Yvonne Sauvageot. Top edges stained red. Shaded blue dust-wrapper, with design in grey and red, printed in blue, red and white on front cover, blue and white on spine with similar design.

On verso of title-page: first edition

[Published: Sept. 20, 1951.]

CONTENTS: Author's Note—Prologue: Mysticism in Man's Life—(Part One: The Cloud and the Fire)—Vision and Illusion—The Problem of Unbelief—On a Dark Night— False Mysticism—Knowledge and Unknowing in Saint John of the Cross—Concepts and Contemplation—The Crisis of Dark Knowledge—(Part Two: Reason and Mysticism in Saint John of the Cross)—The Theological Background—Saint John of the Cross at Salamanca and Alcala —The Battle over the Scriptures—Faith and Reason—Reason in the Life of Contemplation—"Your Reasonable Service"—Between Instinct and Inspiration—Reason and Reasoning—Intelligence in the Prayer of Quiet—(Part Three: Doctrine and Experience)—The Mirror of Silvered Waters —A Dark Cloud Enlightening the Night—The Loving Knowledge of God—To the Mountain and the Hill—The Giant Moves in His Sleep—(Biographical Notes)—Saint Gregory of Nyssa—Saint Bernard of Clairvaux—Saint Thomas of Aquinas—Blessed John Ruysbroeck—Saint Teresa of Avila—Saint John of the Cross—Blaise Pascal—John of Saint Thomas—(Sources)

A16. DEVOTIONS TO ST. JOHN [1953] OF THE CROSS

First edition:

[A Leaflet] DEVOTIONS/in honor of/SAINT JOHN/OF THE CROSS/Feastday—November 24th/[reproduction of St. John of the Cross in supplication]/Compiled by a cloistered Religious/ [Thomas Merton]

8 pp. 13 x 7¾ cm. (no price; n.p., n.d.).

A. Books and Pamphlets

A17. THE SIGN OF JONAS 1953

a. First edition:

THOMAS MERTON/THE SIGN OF JONAS/HARCOURT,
BRACE AND COMPANY/NEW YORK/[ornament]

1 blank leaf, 6 leaves, 3-362 pp., 1 blank leaf. 22 x 14½ cm.
$3.50. Brown cloth with device imprinted in gold on front
cover; lettered in gold on spine; photographed end-papers. Top
edges stained yellow. Brown dust-wrapper printed in green,
white and black on front cover, green and white on spine.
On verso of title-page: first edition
[Published: Feb. 5, 1953.]
> CONTENTS: Prologue—Journey to Nineveh—Solemn Profes-
> sion—Death of an Abbot—Major Orders—To the Altar of
> God—The Whale and the Ivy—The Sign of Jonas—Fire
> Watch, July 4, 1952

b. Paper-back edition:

[Device]/THE SIGN OF JONAS/[device]/by Thomas Merton/
[publisher's symbol]/IMAGE BOOKS/A division of Doubleday
& Company, Inc./Garden City, New York [Image D31.]

352 pp., 4 leaves. 18 x 10½ cm. 95¢. Brown paper printed in
green, white and black on front cover, green and white on
spine.
On verso of title-page: Image Books edition published Feb-
ruary, 1956

A18. BREAD IN THE 1953
WILDERNESS

First edition:

[Title-page adorned with photograph of the Head of Le Devot
Christ upon which is superimposed the title] BREAD IN THE
WILDERNESS [lettered in black reading downward. On verso
of leaf 2, lower case, right corner: symbol of Greek cross com-
posed of the name] Thomas Merton [lettered in black forming

[17]

A. *Books and Pamphlets*

the horizontal arm, and the words] A NEW DIRECTIONS BOOK [lettered in red reading downward forming the vertical arm]

5 leaves, 1-146 pp., 2 blank leaves. 25½ x 21 cm. $6.00. Red cloth with thin-lined indentation of Latin cross extending the width and length of front cover; lettered downward on spine in black. White dust-wrapper is a reproduction of title-page, with addition of author's name printed in black, lower case, and downward on spine in black.

Errata: p. 24, running head (BREAD IN THE WILDERNESS) inverted; p. 30, line 25: "imagination which is no longer able to cope with immaterial" is repeated on line 27; p. 30, line 26: "and which is incapable of the simplest efforts to link two terms of" is repeated on line 28; dust-wrapper, inside back flap, line 20: "analogy" is spelled "anaology"; these errors, with the exception of the misspelled word, have been corrected in the second edition.

Illustrated with photographs of medieval Crucifix at Perpignan, France, which were taken by J. Comet.

[Published: Dec. 23, 1953.]

CONTENTS: Le Devot Christ—Prologue—(Part I: Psalms and Contemplation)—Contemplation in the Liturgy—The Testimony of Tradition—Meanings in Scripture—Songs of the City of God—Errors to Avoid—(Part II: Poetry, Symbolism and Typology)—Poetry, Symbolism and Typology—(Part III: Sacramenta Scripturarum)—Words as Signs and "Sacraments"—Transformation in Discovery—"Visible Mysteries"—"When Israel came out of Egypt"—(Part IV: The Perfect Law of Liberty)—"Thou hast opened my ears"—From Praise to Ecstasy—(Part V: The Shadow of Thy Wings)—Dark Lighting—The Silence of the Psalms—Epilogue—Notes

A. Books and Pamphlets

A19. THE LAST OF THE   1954
FATHERS

First edition:

THOMAS MERTON/The Last of/the Fathers/SAINT BER-
NARD OF CLAIRVAUX AND THE/ENCYCLICAL LET-
TER, DOCTOR MELLIFLUUS/[device]/Harcourt, Brace and
Company/NEW YORK

> 123 pp., 2 blank leaves. 23½ x 14½ cm. $3.50. Green and
> black cloth with device imprinted in silver on front cover;
> lettered downward in silver on spine with design; yellow end-
> papers. Top edges stained yellow. Yellow dust-wrapper, with
> sketch of XIIth century monastery, printed in brown and blue
> on front cover and downward on spine.
>> On verso of title-page: first edition
>> [Published: Je. 3, 1954.]
>>> CONTENTS: Preface—Letter from the Cardinal Protector—
>>> Letter from the Abbot General—The Man and the Saint—
>>> Saint Bernard's Writings—Notes on the Encyclical—Ency-
>>> clical Letter: Doctor Mellifluus—Bibliography—Index

A20.   NO MAN IS AN ISLAND   1955

First edition:

No Man/Is an Island/BY THOMAS MERTON/[design]/Har-
court, Brace and Company/New York

> 4 leaves, ix-xxiii, 1 leaf, 3-264 pp. 21½ x 13½ cm. $3.95.
> Dull royal blue cloth with device imprinted on front cover;
> lettered in silver on spine; grey-blue end-papers. Top edges
> stained grey-blue. Light grey-blue dust-wrapper, with design in
> beige coloring, printed in black and white on front cover and
> spine.
>> On verso of title-page: first edition
>> [Published: Mar. 24, 1955.]
>>> CONTENTS: Author's Note—Prologue—No Man Is An Is-
>>> land—Love Can Be Kept Only by Being Given Away—

A. Books and Pamphlets

Sentences on Hope—Conscience, Freedom, and Prayer—
Pure Intention—The Word of the Cross—Asceticism and
Sacrifice—Being and Doing—Vocation—The Measure of
Charity—Sincerity—Mercy—Recollection—"My Soul Re-
membered God"—The Wind Blows Where It Pleases—The
Inward Solitude—Silence

A21.   THE LIVING BREAD   1956

First edition:

THE/LIVING/BREAD/BY THOMAS MERTON/[quotation
in three lines]/Farrar, Straus & Cudahy · New York [With an
Introduction by Gregory Peter XV Cardinal Agagianian, Patri-
arch of Cilicia and of Armenia.]

3 leaves, v-xxxi, 1 leaf, 3-157 pp. 21 x 13½ cm. $3.00. Marine
blue cloth with device imprinted in gold on front cover; lettered in gold on spine. Top edges stained grey. Marine blue,
mustard shade dust-wrapper, with variations of grey and mosaic
designs of a symbolic figure and chalice, printed in white on
front cover and black and white on spine.

On verso of title-page: First printing, 1956 [Published: Mar.
1, 1956.]

CONTENTS: Introductory Note—Prologue—(I UNTO
THE END)—Christ's Love for Us—Our Response—(II DO
THIS IN MEMORY OF ME)—The Christian Sacrifice
—Worship—Atonement—Agape—(III BEHOLD I AM
WITH YOU)—The Real Presence—Sacramental Contem-
plation—The Soul of Christ in the Eucharist—(IV I AM
THE WAY)—Our Journey to God—The Bread of God—
Communion and Its Effects—(V O SACREM * CONVI-
VIUM)—Come to the Marriage Feast!—The Eucharist and
the Church—"I Have Called You My Friends"—The New
Commandment—Toward the Parousia

---

* This misprint is corrected in the second printing.

B

---◆---

BOOKS WITH CONTRIBUTIONS

BY

THOMAS MERTON

(FOREIGN AND DOMESTIC)

ARRANGED CHRONOLOGICALLY

B. *Contributions to Books*

B1. 1946

[A BRIEF COMMENT ON RELIGIOUS POETRY.] In a New Anthology of Modern Poetry (Revised Edition), edited, and with an Introduction, by Selden Rodman. New York, The Modern Library (Dec.); p. 460. (A Modern Library Giant, #G 46.)

B2. 1949

FOREWORD (scattered excerpts: The Seven Storey Mountain). In Burnt Out Incense, by M. Raymond, O.C.S.O. New York, P. J. Kenedy & Sons (Je.); pp. xi, xii, xiii.

B3. 1949

THE TRAPPISTS GO TO UTAH (see C15); POETRY AND THE CONTEMPLATIVE LIFE (see C14). In the Commonweal Reader, ed. by Edward S. Skillin. New York, Harper & Brothers (Sept.); pp. 13-20, 194-205.

B4. 1950

AN INTRODUCTION. In The City of God, by Saint Augustine. New York, The Modern Library (May); pp. ix-xv. (A Modern Library Giant, #G 74.)

B5. 1950

THE WHITE PEBBLE (see C50). In Where I Found Christ, ed. by John A. O'Brien. New York, Doubleday & Company (Aug.); pp. 235-50.

B6. 1950

STUDENT, MAN-ABOUT-THE-CAMPUS, ATHEIST, TRAPPIST MONK (excerpt: The Seven Storey Mountain). In We

Speak for Ourselves, ed. by Irving Stone. New York, Doubleday & Company (Sept.); pp. [415]-21.

B7.   1951

[A BRIEF COMMENT.] (Back cover of dust-wrapper) for The Pillar of Fire, by Karl Stern. New York, Harcourt, Brace & Company (Feb.).

B8.   1952

THOMAS MERTON/SEEDS OF CONTEMPLATION (excerpt: Seeds of Contemplation). In The Happy Crusaders (A selection of readings affirming the joy of Christianity), compiled by James Edward Tobin. New York, McMullen Books, Incorporated (Ap.); pp. 107-10.

B9.   1952

ST. JOHN OF THE CROSS (see C68). In Saints For Now, ed. by Clare Boothe Luce. New York, Sheed & Ward (Sept.); pp. 250-60 (plus 2 illustrations by Thomas Merton: St. John of the Cross and St. Therese of Lisieux; pp. 248, 280).

B10.   1952

I BEGIN TO MEDITATE (see C30) (excerpt: The Seven Storey Mountain). In The Catholic Digest Reader, selected by the editors of The Catholic Digest. New York, Doubleday & Company (Nov.); pp. [60]-5.

B11.   1953

AUGUST SEVENTH (excerpt: What Are These Wounds?). In Christian Conversation (Catholic Thought for Every Day in the

B. *Contributions to Books*

Year), ed. by Anne Fremantle. New York, Stephen Daye Press (Nov.); p. [199].

B12.   1953

THE CONTEMPLATIVE LIFE CAN BE LED BY ALL (excerpt: Figures for an Apocalypse; from the essay: Poetry and the Contemplative Life). In a Treasury of Catholic Thinking, compiled and edited by Ralph L. Woods. New York, Thomas Y. Crowell Company (Nov.); pp. 346-7.

B13.   1953

INVISIBLE SEEDS; ONE'S OWN VIRTUES (excerpt: Seeds of Contemplation). In The New Treasure Chest, ed. by J. Donald Adams. New York, E. P. Dutton & Company (Nov.); pp. 409-10.

B14.   1953

A FOREWORD (see C74). In St. Bernard of Clairvaux, newly translated and with an introduction by Rev. Bruno Scott James. Chicago, Henry Regnery Company (Nov.); pp. [v]-viii.

B15.   1954

THE PRIMARY APOSTOLATE/THE APOSTOLATE OF PRAYER AND PENANCE. In The National Catholic Almanac [50th Anniversary Edition], compiled by the Franciscan Clerics of Holy Name College, Washington, D. C. Paterson, New Jersey, Saint Anthony's Guild (Jan.); pp. 343-4.

B16.   1954

'TRULY A SUCCESS AS A CISTERCIAN' (excerpt: The Seven Storey Mountain). In The Catholic Bedside Book (An Anthology

[25]

B. *Contributions to Books*

About Catholics and Catholicism), general editor: B. C. L. Keelan. New York, David McKay Company, Incorporated (Jan.); pp. 293-4.

B17.   1954

ART SPEAKS TO A SOUL (excerpt: The Seven Storey Mountain). In The Consolations of Catholicism, compiled and edited by Ralph L. Woods. New York, Appleton-Century-Crofts, Incorporated (Nov.); pp. 106-7.

B18.   1955

O ULTIMO PADRE DA IGREJA (excerpt: The Last of the Fathers). In Perspectivas Dos Estados Unidos—As Artes E As Letras—translated by Adolfo Casais Monteiro. Lisboa, Portugalia Editora (no month); pp. 265-301.

B19.   1955

[Scattered excerpts: Seeds of Contemplation.] In The American Treasury (1455–1955), selected, arranged, and edited by Clifton Fadiman, assisted by Charles Van Doren. New York, Harper & Brothers (Nov.); pp. 680-1.

B20.   1955

THE TRAPPISTS GO TO UTAH (see B3, C15). In The Commonweal Treasury, [which] is made up of selections from The Commonweal Reader (see B3), edited by Edward S. Skillin. New York, The Commonweal Publishing Co., Inc. (Dec.); pp. 116-23.

B21.   1955

PREFACE. In La Vie Eremitique, by Paul Giustiniani. Paris, Editions D'Histoire Et D'Art, Librairie Plon (no month); [7]-18.

B22. 1955

IN SILENTIO [an introduction, translated by Marie Tadié]. In Silence dans le Ciel, a volume of ninety photographs of, with captions by, the monks of La Pierre-qui-vire. This is the First French Edition; the text and photographs are scheduled to appear later under the title "Silence in Heaven" in England and America. Paris, Editions Arthaud (4e trimestre); pp. 12-8, plus 58-9. (The present edition appears both in cloth and paper.)

C

---◆---

CONTRIBUTIONS

BY

THOMAS MERTON

TO NEWSPAPERS AND PERIODICALS,

FOREIGN AND DOMESTIC

The following abbreviations are used: NYHTBR
(New York Herald Tribune Book Review), and
NYTBR (New York Times Book Review).

ARRANGED CHRONOLOGICALLY

C. Newspaper and Periodical Contributions

C1. [A review of] The World's Body. By John Crowe Ransom. *NYHTBR* (May 8, 1938) 10:2.

C2. [A review of] Laughter in the Dark. By Vladimir Nabokoff. *NYHTBR* (May 15, 1938) 10:2.

C3. [A review of] The Enjoyment of Literature. By John Cowper Powys. *NYHTBR* (Nov. 20, 1938) 22:1.

C4. [A review of] Defense of Art. By Christine Herter. *NYHTBR* (Dec. 25, 1938) 12:3.

C5. [A review of] Romanticism and the Gothic Revival. By Agnes Addison. *NYTBR* (Jan. 29, 1939) 4:1.

C6. [A review of] Plato Today. By R. H. S. Crossman. *NYHTBR* (Mar. 19, 1939) 15:1.

C7. [A review of] John Skelton, Laureate. By William Nelson. *NYTBR* (May 28, 1939) 2:2.

C8. [A review of] The Personal Heresy. By E. M. W. Tillyard & C. S. Lewis. *NYTBR* (Jl. 9, 1939) 16:1.

C9. [A review of] Religious Trends in English Poetry (Vol. 1: 1700–1740). By Hoxie Neale Fairchild. *NYHTBR* (Jl. 23, 1939) 17:2.

C10. [A review of] The Burning Oracle. By G. Wilson Knight. *NYTBR* (Sept. 24, 1939) 5:2.

C11. [A review of] D. H. Lawrence and Susan his Cow. By William York Tindall. *NYTBR* (Jan. 4, 1940) 4:1.

C12. Huxley's Pantheon. *The Catholic World,* CLII. 908 (Nov. 1940) [206]-9.

C13. [Mystical Verse, a letter, by Thomas Merton.] The Catholic Poetry Society of America *Bulletin,* IV. 12 (Dec. 1941) 10. [Reply to Clara Hyde's letter in the *Bulletin,* IV. 11 (Oct. 1941) 4, in which she replied to "AN INFORMAL EDITORIAL: IS PRAYER POETRY" in the *Bulletin,* IV. 10 (Aug. 1941) 1.]

C14. Poetry and the Contemplative Life (see A5, B3). *The Commonweal,* XLVI. 12 (Jl. 4, 1947) 280-6.

C15. The Trappists go to Utah (see B3). *The Commonweal,* XLVI. 20 (Aug. 29, 1947) 470-3.

C16. Death of a Trappist. *Integrity,* 2. 2 (Nov. 1947) 3-8.

C17. The Trappists go to Utah (condensed from *Commonweal;* see C15). *The Catholic Digest,* 12. 1 (Nov. 1947) 101-5.

C. *Newspaper and Periodical Contributions*

C18. Active and Contemplative Orders. *The Commonweal,* XLVII. 8 (Dec. 5, 1947) 192-6.

C19. A Christmas Devotion. *The Commonweal,* XLVII. 11 (Dec. 26, 1947) 270-2.

C20. [A review of] I Sing of a Maiden. By Sister M. Therese. *The Commonweal,* XLVII. 19 (Feb. 20, 1948) 477-8.

C21. Death of a Trappist (condensed from *Integrity;* see C16). *The Catholic Digest,* 12. 4 (Feb. 1948) 74-7.

C22. A Trappist Speaks on People, Priests and Prayer. *The Messenger of the Sacred Heart,* LXXXIII. 4 (Ap. 1948) 58-61, plus 89-90.

C23. [A review of] The Third Spiritual Alphabet. By Fray Francisco de Osuna. *The Commonweal,* XLVIII. 4 (May 7, 1948) 85-6.

C24. The Cause of Our Joy (excerpt: Cistercian Contemplatives). *The Catholic World,* CLXVII. 1000 (Jl. 1948) 364-5.

C25. Contemplation in a Rocking Chair. *Integrity,* 2. 11 (Aug. 1948) 15-23.

C26. Schoolboy in England (excerpt: The Seven Storey Mountain). *The Commonweal,* XLVIII. 20 (Aug. 27, 1948) 469-71.

C27. The Sweet Savor of Liberty (excerpt: The Seven Storey Mountain). *The Commonweal,* XLVIII. 23 (Sept. 17, 1948) 541-4.

C28. One Sunday in New York (excerpt: The Seven Storey Mountain). *Information,* LXII. 10 (Oct. 1948) 437-41.

C29. Grace at Work (excerpt: The Seven Storey Mountain; condensed from Information; see C28). *The Catholic Mission Digest,* VI. 10 (Nov. 1948) 8-10.

C30. I Begin to Meditate (see B10) (excerpt: The Seven Storey Mountain). *The Catholic Digest,* 13. 1 (Nov. 1948) 116-20.

C31. The Gift of Understanding. *The Tiger's Eye,* 6. 1 (Dec. 1948) 41-5. (Defunct.)

C32. I Begin to Meditate (Japanese edition; see C30). *The Catholic Digest,* 2. 2 (Feb. 1949) 62-7.

C33. Elected Silence (excerpt: Elected Silence, English version of The Seven Storey Mountain) [in two issues]. [Part 1]

C. *Newspaper and Periodical Contributions*

Foreword by Evelyn Waugh. *The Month,* 1. 3 (Mar. 1949) [158]-79; [Part II] 1. 4 (Ap. 1949) [221]-40.

C34. Poverty (excerpt: Seeds of Contemplation). *The Catholic Worker,* XV. 12 (Ap. 1949) 3:3.

C35. Schoolboy's Lament (excerpt: The Seven Storey Mountain). *The Catholic Digest,* 12. 8 (Je. 1949) 80-2.

C36. Peace That is War (excerpt: Seeds of Contemplation). *The Liguorian,* XXXVII. 7 (Jl. 1949) 431.

C37. PAGE PROOF (a brief excerpt: The Waters of Siloe). *The New York Post* (Sept. 15, 1949) 30:1.

C38. Is Mysticism Normal? *The Commonweal,* LI. 4 (Nov. 4, 1949) 94-8.

C39. Trappists Make Silent Martyrs (excerpt: The Waters of Siloe). *The Catholic Digest,* 14. 1 (Nov. 1949) 29-36.

C40. The Contemplative Life/Its Meaning and Necessity. *The Dublin Review,* 446 (Winter 1949) 26-35.

C41. First Christmas at Gethsemani (unpublished material from the original Ms. of The Seven Storey Mountain); introductory comment by Sister M. Therese Lentfoehr, S.D.S. *The Catholic World,* CLXX. 1017 (Dec. 1949) [166]-73.

C42. [An offprint of] THE TRANSFORMING UNION/IN ST. BERNARD AND ST. JOHN OF THE CROSS. Extrait des—*Collectanea Ordinis Cisterciensium Reformatorum*—(in five issues) avril et juillet 1948, pp. [107]-117 et [210]-223; janvier et octobre 1949, pp. [41]-52 et [353]-361; janvier 1950, pp. [25]-38.

C43. September, 1949 (later enlarged and included in The Sign of Jonas). *The Month,* 3. 2 (Feb. 1950) [107]-13.

C44. Self-Denial and the Christian. *The Commonweal,* LI. 25 (Mar. 31, 1950) [649]-53.

C45. The Primacy of Contemplation. *Cross and Crown,* II. I (Mar. 1950) 3-16.

C46. Todo y Nada/Writing and Contemplation (unpublished material on Writing and Contemplation from the original Ms. of The Seven Storey Mountain); introductory comment by Sister M. Therese Lentfoehr, S.D.S. *Renascence,* II. 2 (Spring 1950) 87-101.

C47. Un Americano A Roma (excerpt: La Montagna Dalle Sette

C. Newspaper and Periodical Contributions

Balze, Italian version of The Seven Storey Mountain). *L'Osservatore Romano* (28 Aprile 1950) 3:2.

C48. N.D. Gethsemani [Chronique: Annual Report, Gethsemani; written in French] (Kentucky, Etats-Unis). *Collectanea Ordinis Cisterciensium Reformatorum,* XII. 2 (Ap. 1950) 132-4.

C49. I Will be Your Monk (unpublished material on St. Therese of the Child Jesus from the original Ms. of The Seven Storey Mountain); introductory comment by Sister M. Therese Lentfoehr, S.D.S. *The Catholic World,* CLXXI. 1022 (May 1950) [86]-93.

C50. The White Pebble (later enlarged and included in Where I Found Christ; see B5). *The Sign,* 29. 12 (Jl. 1950) 26-8, plus 69.

C51. The Psalms and Contemplation [in three issues] (later enlarged and included in Bread in the Wilderness). *Orate Fratres* (now Worship), XXIV. 8 (Jl. 1950) 341-7; [Part II] XXIV. 9 (Aug. 1950) 385-91; [Part III] XXIV. 10 (Sept. 1950) 433-40.

C52. Thomas Merton on Renunciation (unpublished material from the original Ms. of The Seven Storey Mountain); introductory comment by Sister M. Therese Lentfoehr, S.D.S. *The Catholic World,* CLXXI. 1026 (Sept. 1950) [420]-9.

C53. Le Moine Et Le Chasseur. *Dieu Vivant,* 17 ([Fourth] Trimestre–1950), [93]-8.

C54. Father Merton Denies Rumors. *The Catholic World,* CLXXII. 1032 (Mar. 1951) iv.

C55. Monks and Hunters (American version of Le Moine Et Le Chasseur; see C53). *The Commonweal,* LIV. 2 (Ap. 20, 1951) 39-40.

C56. N.D. Gethsemani [Chronique: Annual Report, Gethsemani; written in French] (Kentucky, Etats-Unis). *Collectanea Ordinis Cisterciensium Reformatorum,* XIII. 2 (Ap. 1951) 141-2.

C57. Etapes De Mon Chemin Vers Dieu (excerpt: La Nuit Privee D'Etoiles, French version of The Seven Storey Mountain). *La Vie Spirituelle,* 365 (Aout-Septembre 1951) [161]-71.

C. *Newspaper and Periodical Contributions*

C58. The Ascent to Truth (excerpt: The Ascent to Truth). *Thought*, XXVI. 102 (Autumn 1951) [361]-83.

C59. How to Believe in God (excerpt: The Ascent to Truth). *The Catholic Digest*, 16. 3 (Jan. 1952) 41-4.

C60. Christ Suffers Again. *Action Now!*, 5. 5 (Mar. 1952) 13.

C61. N.D. Gethsemani [Chronique: Annual Report, Gethsemani; written in French] (Kentucky, Etats-Unis). *Collectanea Ordinis Cisterciensium Reformatorum*, XIV. 2 (Ap. 1952) [143]-4.

C62. Le Sacrement De L'Avent/Dans La Spiritualite/De Saint Bernard. *Dieu Vivant*, 23 ([First] Trimestre–1953), [21]-43.

C63. PAGE PROOF (a brief excerpt: The Sign of Jonas). *The New York Post* (Feb. 5, 1953) 18:1.

C64. The Sign of Jonas (excerpt: The Sign of Jonas). *This Week Magazine* (Mar. 8, 1953), 18, plus 30, plus 43, plus 50.

C65. Les Psaumes Et La Contemplation (French version of The Psalms and Contemplation; see C51). *Masses Ouvrieres*, 9. 85 (Avril 1953) 35-60.

C66. Saint Bernard: Monk and Apostle/Reflections in his Eighth Centenary Year * [in two issues]. *The Tablet*, 201. 5896 (May 23, 1953) 438-9; [Part II] 201. 5897 (May 30, 1953) 466-7.

C67. PAGE PROOF (a brief excerpt: Seeds of Contemplation). *The New York Post* (Je. 16, 1953) 24:1.

C68. St. John of the Cross. *Perspectives* USA, 4 (Summer 1953) [52]-61 (reprinted from Saints For Now; see B9).

C69. St. John of the Cross. *Perspectives* [British edition; see C68], 4 (Summer 1953) [52]-61.

C70. San Giovanni Della Croce. *Prospetti* [Italian edition; see C68], 4 (Summer 1953) [67]-76.

C71. Der Heilige Johannes Vom Kreuz. *Perspektiven* [German edition; see C68], 4 (Summer 1953) [53]-62.

---

* This article first appeared in French as the Preface to a biography of Saint Bernard and published by the Cistercian Order in commemoration of the eighth centenary of the saint's death. Frater Louis's superiors desired him to make an exception to his present practice of not writing for magazines, in allowing this article to be printed here. It was also published in America; see C75.

C. Newspaper and Periodical Contributions

C72. Saint Bernard Et L'Amerique (excerpt: Aux Sources Du Silence, French version of The Waters of Siloe). [The first page of this article is new, the rest follows the text.] *Temoignages,* 38-39 (Juillet 1953) [89]-98.

C73. PAGE PROOF (a brief excerpt: Seeds of Contemplation). *The New York Post* (Jl. 30, 1953) 20:1.

C74. Bernard of Clairvaux (excerpt: A Foreword, in St. Bernard of Clairvaux; see B14). *Jubilee,* 1. 4 (Aug. 1953) 33.

C75. St. Bernard, Monk and Apostle. *Cross and Crown,* V. 3 (Sept. 1953) 251-63.

C76. The Psalms as Poetry (excerpt: Bread in the Wilderness). *The Commonweal,* LIX. 4 (Oct. 30, 1953) 79-81.

C77. O Diario De Thomas Merton (excerpt: The Sign of Jonas). *A Ordem,* L. 4 (Outbubro 1953) 17-25.

C78. PAGE PROOF (a brief excerpt: Bread in the Wilderness). *The New York Post* (Dec. 22, 1953) 28:1.

C79. [An offprint of] ACTION AND CONTEMPLATION/IN ST. BERNARD. Extrait des—*Collectanea Ordinis Cisterciensium Reformatorum*—(in three issues) janvier et juillet 1953, pp. [26]-31 et [203]-216; avril 1954, pp. [105]-121.

C80. N.D. Gethsemani [Chronique: Annual Report, Gethsemani; written in French] (Kentucky, Etats-Unis). *Collectanea Ordinis Cisterciensium Reformatorum,* XVI. 2 (Ap. 1954) [145].

C81. Nel Deserto. *Camaldoli,* IX. 40 (Gennaio-Marzo 1955) 1-5.

C82. Reality, Art, and Prayer (excerpt: No Man Is An Island). *The Commonweal,* LXI. 25 (Mar. 23, 1955) 658-9.

C83. Dans Le Desert De Dieu. *Temoignages,* 48 (mars 1955) [132]-6.

C84. PAGE PROOF (a brief excerpt: No Man Is An Island). *The New York Post* (Mar. 28, 1955) 24:1.

C85. You and I (a brief excerpt: No Man Is An Island). *Books on Trial,* XIII. 6 (Ap. 1955) 311.

C86. N.D. Gethsemani [Chronique: Annual Report, Gethsemani; written in French] (Kentucky, Etats-Unis). *Collectanea Ordinis Cisterciensium Reformatorum,* XVII. 2 (Ap. 1955) [21].

C. *Newspaper and Periodical Contributions*

C87. Something to Live For (a brief excerpt: No Man Is An Island). *NYTBR* (May 15, 1955) 2:5.

C88. PAGE PROOF (a brief excerpt: No Man Is An Island). *The New York Post* (Je. 19, 1955) 8m:1.

C89. PAGE PROOF (a brief excerpt: No Man Is An Island). *The New York Post* (Je. 21, 1955) 28:1.

C90. Le Recueillement (excerpt: No Man Is An Island). *Temoignages* (Juillet 1955) [321]-30.

C91. PAGE PROOF (a brief excerpt: No Man Is An Island). *The New York Post* (Aug. 29, 1955) 24:1.

C92. Raccoglimento. *Camaldoli,* IX. 42 (Luglio-Settembre 1955) 81-8.

C93. Praying the Psalms (excerpt: Praying the Psalms *). *Worship,* XXIX. 8 (Sept. 1955) 481-3.

C94. THE TOWER OF BABEL. *Jubilee, 3.* 6 (Oct. 1955) [21-35].

C95. [An offprint of] THE CHRISTMAS SERMONS OF BL. GUERRIC. Extrait des—*Collectanea Ordinis Cisterciensium Reformatorum*—(oct.-dec. 1955) [229]-44.

---

* A pamphlet. To be published in 1956 by the Liturgical Press, Collegeville, Minnesota.

D

CRITICAL ARTICLES AND LETTERS

ABOUT THOMAS MERTON

IN PERIODICALS, NEWSPAPERS

AND BOOKS

(Foreign and Domestic)

ARRANGED CHRONOLOGICALLY

D. *Critical Articles About Thomas Merton*

D1. [Essay-Review *: THIRTY POEMS.] The Verses of Thomas Merton, [by] Robert Lowell. *The Commonweal,* XLII. 10 (Je. 22, 1945) 240-2.

D2. [Essay-Review: THIRTY POEMS.] "NEW DIREC-TIONS"/PRESENTS A CATHOLIC POET, [by] Sister Julie, O.P. *America,* LXXIII. 16 (Jl. 21, 1945) 316-8.

D3. The Poet Turned Monk/(To Thomas Merton), [a poem,] by George A. McCauliff. *Spirit,* XII. 3 (Jl. 1945) 72-3.

D4. [Essay-Review: THIRTY POEMS.] Modern or Medieval-ist?, by Louise T. Nicholl. *The Saturday Review of Literature,* XXIX. 12 (Mar. 23, 1946) 44.

D5. [Essay-Review: A MAN IN THE DIVIDED SEA.] A Poet of Genuine Talent, by John Frederick Nims. *The Saturday Review of Literature,* XXIX. 43 (Oct. 26, 1946) 36.

D6. [Essay-Review: A MAN IN THE DIVIDED SEA.] A Trap-pist Canticle, by John Nerber. *Poetry,* LXIX. 111 (Dec. 1946) 165-8.

D7. Thomas Merton: Poet, by Speer Strahan. *The Ave Maria,* 65 (n.s.). 8 (Feb. 22, 1947) 231-4.

D8. Poetry and Contemplation [a letter, reply to Poetry and the Contemplative Life; see C14], by Mary Ellen Evans. *The Commonweal,* XLVI. 16 (Aug. 1, 1947) 383-4.

D9. A Christmas Meditation [a letter, reply to A Christmas De-votion; see C19], by Barry Gill. *The Commonweal,* XLVII. 14 (Jan. 16, 1948) 349.

D10. TOAST OF THE AVANT-GARDE: A TRAPPIST POET, by Will Lissner. *The Catholic World,* CLXI. 995 (Feb. 1948) [424]-32.

D11. [Essay-Review: A MAN IN THE DIVIDED SEA.] Of Thomas Merton:/His Word and His Spirit, by Frank J. Wiess. *The Carroll Quarterly,* 1. 2 (Spring 1948) 4-13.

D12. Thomas Merton. In Return to Tradition [a brief critical piece; see G32], by Francis B. Thornton (Ap. 1948); p. 850.

D13. [Essay-Review: FIGURES FOR AN APOCALYPSE.]

---

* I have listed in this section a number of Essay-Reviews which, in my opinion, would be of value to the student and reader of this Bibliography; the task of inclusion and exclusion was not an easy one.

D. Critical Articles About Thomas Merton

Prophecy for the Atomic Age, by Sister M. Madeleva, C.S.C. *Books on Trial*, VII. 2 (Jl.-Aug. 1948) 63.

D14. Mystics Among Us. *Time*, LII. 15 (Oct. 11, 1948) 87-9.

D15. [A review of] THE SEVEN STOREY MOUNTAIN, [by] Sterns Cunningham. *Newsletter*, Catholic Book Club, XL. 3 (Oct. 1948) [1].

D16. [Essay-Review: THE SEVEN STOREY MOUNTAIN.] Exciting Autobiography/Condemns Modernism, by Helene Magaret, Ph.D. *Books on Trial*, VII. 4 (Oct.-Nov. 1948) 133, plus 144.

D17. White Man's Culture. *Time*, LII. 22 (Nov. 29, 1948) 81-2.

D18. St. Malachy, by Hayden Carruth. A Critical Supplement to Poetry (Feb. 1949), 10-3; refers analytically to St. Malachy, a poem by Thomas Merton which first appeared in *Poetry* (see G41).

D19. [Essay-Review: THE SEVEN STOREY MOUNTAIN.] The Complete Twentieth-Century Man, by Francis X. Connolly. *Thought*, XXIV. 92 (Mar. 1949) 10-4.

D20. The Mountain. *Time*, LIII. 15 (Ap. 11, 1949) 62-3.

D21. Thomas Merton/Poet of the Contemplative Life, by James A. Thielen. *The Catholic World*, CLXIX. 1010 (May 1949) [86]-90.

D22. Trappist Monastery/It Offers The Strict Life Described In "Seven Storey Mountain"; [plus] Merton Likes Monastery/ But He Has Reservations. *Life*, 26. 21 (May 23, 1949) 84-90.

D23. Catholic Author of the Month/Thomas Merton, Brother Louis, O.C.S.O., 1915–, by T. Tobin. *The Liguorian*, XXXVII. 7 (Jl. 1949) 443-4.

D24. Merton: His Problem and a Solution, by Gervase Toelle, O.Carm. *Spirit*, XVI. 3 (Jl. 1949) 84-9.

D25. [Essay-Review: ELECTED SILENCE, English version of Seven Storey Mountain.] Books in General [Elected Silence], by V. S. Pritchett. *The New Statesman and Nation*, XXXVIII. 962 (Aug. 13, 1949) 174, plus 176. (Mr. Pritchett's essay-article resulted in a heated exchange of correspondence that ran in six issues.) Elected Silence [a letter, reply to Mr. Pritchett], by Evelyn Waugh. XXXVIII. 963 (Aug. 20, 1949) 197; Elected Silence [a letter, reply to Mr.

D. Critical Articles About Thomas Merton

Waugh], by R. van Eyck. XXXVIII. 964 (Aug. 27, 1949)
220; Elected Silence [two letters, replies to Mr. R. van
Eyck and Mr. Waugh], by Evelyn Waugh and Harold
Binns. XXXVIII. 965 (Sept. 3, 1949) 245-6; Elected Silence
[two letters, replies to Mr. Waugh and Mr. Binns], by V. S.
Pritchett and Evelyn Waugh. XXXVIII. 966 (Sept. 10,
1949) 274; Elected Silence [two letters, replies to Mr.
Waugh and Mr. Pritchett], by R. van Eyck and Evelyn
Waugh. XXXVIII. 967 (Sept. 17, 1949) 302.

D26. [Essay-Review: SEEDS OF CONTEMPLATION.] The
Fruits of Mysticism, by Y. H. Krikorian. *The New Repub-
lic,* 121. 11 (Sept. 12, 1949) 17-8.

D27. Action and Contemplation, [by] James M. Gillis, C.S.P.
Cross and Crown, 1. 3 (Sept. 1949) 245-60.

D28. [Essay-Review: THE WATERS OF SILOE.] Thomas Merton, Trappist. *Newsweek,* XXXIV. 12 (Sept. 19, 1949) 72-3.

D29. Elected Silence [a letter, reply to Mr. Waugh; see D25], by
V. S. Pritchett. *The New Statesman and Nation,* XXXVIII.
969 (Oct. 1, 1949) 358.

D30. [A review of] THE WATERS OF SILOE, [by Harold C.
Gardiner]. *Newsletter,* Catholic Book Club, XLI. 6 (Oct.
1949) [1].

D31. [A letter, reply to Gervase Toelle, O.Carm.; see D24.] By
Sister Mary Catherine, O.S.U. *Spirit,* XVI. 5 (Nov. 1949)
162.

D32. [Essay-Review: THE WATERS OF SILOE.] The Cistercians, by Joseph McSorley. *The Catholic World,* CLXX.
1017 (Dec. 1949) [198]-203.

D33. [Essay-Review: THE TEARS OF THE BLIND LIONS.]
Merton's Most Recent Poems, by Gervase Toelle, O.Carm.
Spirit, XVI. 6 (Jan. 1950) 195-7.

D34. [Essay-Review: DER BERG DER SIEBEN STUFEN.] Der
Fall Thomas Merton, by Heinz Politzer. *Die Neue Rund-
schau,* 61. 1 (Erstes Heft, 1950) 131-5.

D35. La Conversion Et L'Ordination De Thomas Merton, by
Chanoine Francois Delteil. *Echos De Noble-Val,* 148 (Jan-
vier-Fevrier-Mars 1950) 7-10.

D36. Two Letters on "The Merton Problem" [replies to Gervase

D. *Critical Articles About Thomas Merton*

Toelle, O.Carm.; see D33, D24], by Sister M. Therese Lentfoehr, S.D.S., and Eric Bruno, O.F.M. *Spirit*, XVII. 1 (Mar. 1950) 20-5.

D37. [Two letters on "The Merton Problem", replies to Eric Bruno, by] Margery Mansfield (see D36), [to Sister M. Therese Lentfoehr, Gervase Toelle, Eric Bruno, by] George A. McCauliff (see D36, D33, D24). *Spirit*, XVII. 2 (May 1950) 62-3.

D38. Merton and the Critics, by Gervase Toelle, O.Carm. *Renascence*, II. 2 (Spring 1950) 139-46.

D39. Thomas Merton: poet/of contemplation, [by] Sister M. Joselyn. *America*, 83. 16 (Jl. 22, 1950) 420-2.

D40. A Commentary Note on "The Merton Problem" [addressed to Sister M. Therese Lentfoehr], by Sister Mary Irma (see D37). The Catholic Poetry Society of America *Bulletin*, VI. 16 (Aug. 1950) 2-3.

D41. [Essay-Review: LA MONTAGNA DALLE SETTE BALZE, Italian version of The Seven Storey Mountain.] La Tua Solitudine Portera Frutti Immensi, by D. Mondrone, S.I. *Civilta Cattolica*, III. 2403 (5 Agosto 1950) [272]-84.

D42. Thomas Merton/Poeta Della Contemplazione. *L'Osservatore Romano* (4 Novembre 1950) 4:2.

D43. Moisson De Silence, by Helene Lubienska De Lenval. *La Vie Spirituelle*, 363 (Juin 1951) [616]-27.

D44. [Essay-Review: SELECTED POEMS OF THOMAS MERTON; see F2.] Thomas Merton as a Poet/Form and Content, by I. T. Quin. *The Irish Monthly*, LXXIX. 939 (Sept. 1951) 381-4.

D45. Poetry in Education, by Sister M. Therese Lentfoehr, S.D.S. *Spirit*, XVIII. 4 (Sept. 1951) 113-22. (Paper delivered at The Catholic Poetry Society Congress on Poetry, Hunter College of New York City, April 14, 1951.)

D46. [Essay-Review: THE ASCENT TO TRUTH.] "If You Are Looking . . ./Look Inside Yourself", by Sister M. Therese Lentfoehr, S.D.S. *Books on Trial*, X. 2 (Oct. 1951) 66-7.

D47. [A review of] THE ASCENT TO TRUTH, [by] Rt. Rev.

D. *Critical Articles About Thomas Merton*

Joseph M. Egan. Catholic Book Club/*News*[letter], XLIII. 12 (Oct. 1951) [1-2].

D48. Le Cardinal Et Le Trappists/Aspects Du Catholicisme Aux Etats-Unis, by Antoine Lauras. *Etudes,* 271 (Dec. 1951) [368]-78.

D49. [Essay-Review: THE ASCENT TO TRUTH.] Everyman's Vocation/Father Merton's Introduction to Mystical Theology, by T. S. Gregory. *The Tablet,* 198. 5823 (Dec. 29, 1951) 489-90.

D50. The Poetry of Thomas Merton, by Sister M. Madeleva, C.S.C. In From an Abundant Spring (The Walter Farrell Memorial Volume of *The Thomist*), edited by the staff of *The Thomist.* New York, P. J. Kenedy & Sons (Nov. 24, 1952); pp. 525-34.

D51. THOMAS MERTON/A Modern Man in Reverse, by [Dom] Aelred Graham, [O.S.B.]. *The Atlantic Monthly,* 191. 1 (Jan. 1953) 70-4.

D52. Benedictine v[ersus] Trappist. *Time,* LXI. 5 (Feb. 2, 1953) 72, plus 74.

D53. The meaning of/Thomas Merton, [by] Joseph Landy. *America,* 88. 21 (Feb. 21, 1953) 569-70.

D54. [Essay-Review: THE SIGN OF JONAS.] In the Belly of a Paradox, by Ben Ray Redman. *The Saturday Review,* XXXVI. 8 (Feb. 21, 1953) 45-6.

D55. [Essay-Review: THE SIGN OF JONAS.] From the Belly of the Whale, by Henry Rago. *The Commonweal,* LVII. 21 (Feb. 27, 1953) 526-9.

D56. [Essay-Review: THE SIGN OF JONAS.] "Something of a Monk's Spiritual Life and of/His Thoughts in Terms of Personal Experience", by Bernard Theall, O.S.B. *Books on Trial,* XI. 5 (Mar. 1953) 189, plus 208.

D57. In Defense of Thomas Merton [a letter, reply to Aelred Graham; see D51], by S. Earle Dubbel. *The Atlantic Monthly,* 191. 3 (Mar. 1953) 20.

D58. [A review of] THE SIGN OF JONAS, [by] Harold C. Gardiner, S.J. Catholic Book Club/*News*[letter], XLV. 5 (Mar. 1953) [1-2].

D. *Critical Articles About Thomas Merton*

D59. Thomas Merton and/Dom Aelred Graham, [by] William Davey. *Integrity,* 7. 7 (Ap. 1953) 34-42.

D60. Fr. Thomas Merton on the Monastic Life [a letter, reply to Saint Bernard: Monk and Apostle/Reflections in his Eighth Centenary Year; see C66], by E. B. Young. *The Tablet,* 201. 5898 (Je. 6, 1953) 500.

D61. [Essay-Review: THE SIGN OF JONAS.] O Diario Sem Tempo, by D. Timoteo Amoroso Anastacio, O.S.B. *A Ordem,* L. 2 (Agosto 1953) 4-8.

D62. [Essay-Review: THE SIGN OF JONAS.] Merton's Jonas, by Sister M. Therese Lentfoehr, S.D.S. *Renascence,* VI. 1 (Autumn 1953) 44-52.

D63. O Diario De Thomas Merton, by D. Basilio Penido, O.S.B. *A Ordem,* L. 4 (Outbubro 1953) 14-7.

D64. THOMAS MERTON AND HIS CRITICS/An Essay in Interpretation, [by] Dom Denys Rutledge, [O.S.B.]. *The Clergy Review,* XXXVIII. II (Nov. 1953) 671-8.

D65. Poete Et Trappiste/Thomas Merton, by Robert Kothen. In Convertis Du XXe Siecle (Premier Volume), Collection Dirigee Par F. Lelotte, S.J. Paris, Casterman (1954); pp. [135]-50.

D66. [Essay-Review: LA MANNE DU DESERT OU LE MYS-TERE DES PSAUMES.] Le Pain Des Psaumes, by Helene Lubienska De Lenval. *La Vie Spirituelle,* 400 (Novembre 1954) [410]-2.

D67. [Essay-Review: BREAD IN THE WILDERNESS.] Flash of Dark Lightning, by Sister M. Therese Lentfoehr, S.D.S. *Renascence,* VII. 2 (Winter 1954) 103-8.

D68. A BIBLIOGRAPHY OF/THOMAS MERTON, compiled by Frank Dell'Isola. *Thought,* XXIX. 115 (Winter 1954–1955) [574]-96.

D69. Thomas Merton/and T. S. Eliot, [by] Sister Mary Julian Baird, R.S.M. *America,* 92. 17 (Jan. 22, 1955) 424-6.

D70. Action and Contemplation in St. Bernard. *Theology Digest,* III. 2 (Spring 1955) [100].

D71. [Essay-Review: NO MAN IS AN ISLAND.] Notes and Meditations/by Thomas Merton, by Sister M. Therese Lentfoehr, S.D.S. *Books on Trial,* XIII. 6 (Ap. 1955) 311-2.

D. *Critical Articles About Thomas Merton*

D72. [A review of] NO MAN IS AN ISLAND, [by] Harold C. Gardiner. Catholic Book Club *Newsletter,* XLVII. 6 (Ap. 1955) [1-2].

D73. [Essay-Review: NO MAN IS AN ISLAND.] The Mysticism of Thomas Merton, [by] Aelred Graham. *The Commonweal,* LXII. 6 (May 13, 1955) 155-9.

D74. A Journey to Gethsemani, by Frank Dell'Isola. *Cross and Crown,* VIII. 3 (Sept. 1956).

E

TRANSLATIONS

BY

THOMAS MERTON

E1. THE KINGDOM OF JESUS 1946

THE LIFE AND THE KINGDOM/OF JESUS/IN CHRIS-
TIAN SOULS/A TREATISE ON CHRISTIAN PERFEC-
TION/FOR USE BY CLERGY OR LAITY/BY/SAINT JOHN
EUDES/Translated from the French by/A Trappist Father
[Thomas Merton] in/The Abbey of Our Lady of Gethsemani/
With an Introduction by/THE RIGHT REVEREND/MON-
SIGNOR [now Bishop] FULTON J. SHEEN/[publisher's de-
vice]/NEW YORK/P. J. KENEDY & SONS

> 3 leaves, v-xxxv, 1 leaf, 3-348 pp. 21 x 14½ cm. $3.00. Navy
> blue cloth with device imprinted in gold on front cover; let-
> tered in gold on spine. Bright blue dust-wrapper, with medal-
> lion of St. John Eudes, printed in black on front cover and
> spine.
> [Published: Ap. 10, 1946.]

E2. THE SOUL OF 1946
THE APOSTOLATE

The Soul/of the/Apostolate/By/Dom Jean-Baptiste Chautard,
O.C.S.O./(Abbot of Notre Dame de Sept-Fons)/55TH THOU-
SAND/in U. S. A./Complete new translation/by/A Monk
[Thomas Merton] of Our Lady of Gethsemani

> 2 leaves, [v]-xxii, 1 leaf, [1]-290 pp., 1 leaf, 2 blank leaves.
> 18 x 12 cm. $3.00. Black leather lettered in gold on front cover
> and downward on spine. No dust-wrapper. Edges stained red.
> [Published: Sept. 16, 1946, by the Monks of Our Lady of
> Gethsemani, Trappist, Kentucky.]

E3. THE SPIRIT OF SIMPLICITY 1948

The Cistercian Library. No. 3./The/Spirit of Simplicity/ Char-
acteristic of the Cistercian Order/An Official Report,/ demanded
and approved by the /GENERAL CHAPTER/Together with

E. *Translations by Thomas Merton*

Texts from/ST. BERNARD OF CLAIRVAUX/on Interior Simplicity/Translation and Commentary by/A Cistercian Monk [Thomas Merton] of Our Lady of Gethsemani/TRAPPIST, KENTUCKY/1948

4 leaves, ii-[vii], [1]-139 pp., 1 blank leaf. 18½ x 12 cm. $1.75. Black cloth lettered in gold on front cover and downward on spine. No dust-wrapper.

Illustrated with 12 sepia photographs of ancient and modern Cistercian architecture which were taken by Jahan and Sauvageot, and a detailed sketch, with explanatory notes, of a typical Cistercian abbey in the 12th century.

[Published: Ap. 23, 1948, by the Monks of Our Lady of Gethsemani, Trappist, Kentucky.]

F

---◆---

MISCELLANEA

SPECIAL FOREIGN EDITIONS

RECORDINGS

F. *Miscellanea*

F1.   THE WATERS OF SILENCE   1950

First English de Luxe edition:

THE WATERS/OF SILENCE/[English version of The Waters of Siloe; see All.]/by/THOMAS MERTON/With a Foreword by/Evelyn Waugh/[device]/THEODORE BRUN LIMITED, LONDON/98, Great Russell Street, W.C.1

6 leaves, 3-299 pp. 22½ x 15½ cm. 32s. Black leather with design by George Motte imprinted in gold on front cover; lettered in gold on spine; photographed end-papers by Yvonne Sauvageot. Top edges stained gold. No dust-wrapper.

36 photographs.

On verso of title-page: This Limited de Luxe Edition is published/by special arrangement with Messrs. Hollis &/ Carter, Ltd., London, and appears simultane-/ously with their first edition. One hundred/and twenty copies have been printed for sale. In/addition, five copies, numbered I to V, have/been struck off as presentation and reference/copies./No. 86 [written in ink]

[Published: Jl. 21, 1950.]

This version, as in the Hollis and Carter issue, has deletions of sections and transpositions of chapters, e.g., the "Prologue" and a "Note on the Function of a Contemplative Order" which comprise the beginning in the American edition are eliminated. The title heading of Chapter I in the two English and American editions is similar, but Chapter II of the English editions reads: "Cistercian Life in the Twelfth Century," which in the American edition is Chapter XII. In the latter edition, Chapter II reads: "De Rance and La Trappe," which in the English editions becomes Chapter III. From here on the original sequence of chapter headings follows; however, Chapter XIII of the American edition which reads: "The Cistercian Character and Sanctity," has been entirely omitted in the English editions. Thus Chapter XIII in the latter editions reads: "Paradisus Claustralis," which in the American edition is Chapter XIV. This is followed by an Appendix, e.g., "The Daily Life of a Cistercian in our Time" (in the

American edition it was appended after the "Table of Contents"), a "Bibliography" and an "Index"; the "Glossary of Some Monastic Terms" is not included.

F2. SELECTED POEMS OF 1950
THOMAS MERTON

First English edition:

SELECTED/POEMS/BY/THOMAS MERTON/WITH A FOREWORD BY/ROBERT SPEAIGHT/LONDON/HOLLIS & CARTER/1950

2 leaves, v-xii, 1 leaf, 3-113 pp., 1 blank leaf. 22½ x 15 cm. 12/6. Sand colored cloth lettered upward in gold on green rectangle on spine. Top edges stained green. Chartreuse dustwrapper printed in maroon with design.

[Published: Nov. 29, 1950.]

CONTENTS: Excerpts from Merton's four books of poetry: 14 from THIRTY POEMS; 25 from A MAN IN THE DIVIDED SEA; 15 from FIGURES FOR AN APOCALYPSE; 11 from THE TEARS OF THE BLIND LIONS. Included in this collection is a hitherto unpublished poem: SPORTS WITHOUT BLOOD/A Letter to [the late] Dylan Thomas (see D44, G52).

RECORDINGS

(To date only two records have been cut which relate to Thomas Merton:)

F3. The Harvard Vocarium Records: 1950 (78 RPM, 1 12″ record, #L 1018; 2 sides). A reading of his selected verse by Robert Speaight. Side 1: The Trappist Cemetery (from A Man in the Divided Sea); side 2: Band 1: In the Rain and the Sun; Band 2: A Psalm (from The Tears of the Blind Lions).

F4. Columbia Masterworks: Ap. 2, 1951 (LP, 33⅓ RPM, 1 12″ record, #ML 54394; 2 sides) [also supplied in 78 RPM, 4

F. Miscellanea

12" records, #MM 1021]. Side 1: Laudate Dominum: Gregorian Chant by the Trappist Monks of the Abbey of Gethsemani, Kentucky; side 2: Laudes Vespertinae: Hymns in Honor of the Blessed Virgin Mary; with program notes by Thomas Merton.*

LAUDATE DOMINUM: Band 1: Exsurge (Introit for Septuagesima)—Band 2: Lutum Fecit (Communion, Antiphon for the Mass of Wed. after IV Lent)—Band 3: Quinque Prudentes (From Common Mass of Virgins)—Band 4: Puer (Introit of the Principal Mass of Christmas)—Band 5: Vox in Rama (Communion Antiphon of Holy Innocents)—Band 6: Videns Dominus (Communion of Mass for the Sat. after IV Lent)—Band 7: Collegerunt (Responsory from the Palm Sun. Procession)—Band 8: Nemo Te (Communion of the Mass for Sat. after III Lent)—Band 9: Mane Nobiscum (Antiphon from the Corpus Christi Office)—Band 10: Dirigatur (Gradual of Mass for Tue. after I Lent)—Band 11: Beatus Bernardus (Cistercian Responsory for the Feast of St. Bernard)
LAUDES VESPERTINAE: Band 1: Ave Maria—Band 2: Magnificat—Band 3: Ego Dormio—Band 4: Salve Mater Misericordiae—Band 5: Tota Pulchra Es—Band 6: Rosa Vernans —Band 7: Salve Regina (Hymn to the Blessed Virgin Mary sung ["after Compline" †])

---

* When this record was issued, it was erroneously believed (and still is) that the running commentary was the voice of Thomas Merton; actually, the voice used is that of another member of the Gethsemani community.

† This, according to a note from Thomas Merton, is more exact and to the point than the actual wording on the slip-case: ". . . sung at the conclusion of the Divine Office."

G

---◆---

THE POETRY OF THOMAS MERTON
IN PERIODICALS,
NEWSPAPERS AND BOOKS

The following abbreviations are used:
TP (Thirty Poems); AMITDS (A Man in the
Divided Sea); FFAA (Figures for an Apocalypse),
and TTOTBL (The Tears of the Blind Lions).

ARRANGED CHRONOLOGICALLY

G. *The Poetry of Thomas Merton*

(In the main body of the bibliography the only allusion to Merton's poetry was in listing and describing his five books * of verse. On advisement I did not list the individual appearance of his poems which began appearing in anthologies, newspapers and magazines from 1939 to 1955, but immediately after publication of the bibliography in *Thought,*† a separate listing of Merton's verse was deemed essential to the bibliographical researcher and thesis writer.)

G1. FABLE FOR A WAR ‡; AUBADE: BERMUDA; LIT-ANY; BUREAUCRATS: DIGGERS; THESE YEARS A WINTER; CHRISTMAS AS TO PEOPLE. In Columbia Poetry [an anthology of Columbia students' verse], with an Introduction by Charles Hanson Towne. New York, Columbia University Press (Je. 1939); pp. 60-1, 62, 63, 64, 65, 66-7. (None of these poems appear in his books of poetry.)

G2. [Second appearance of] Fable for a War (excerpt: Columbia Poetry; see G1). *The New York Times* (Je. 18, 1939) 36:6.

G3. [First appearance of] Song (in AMITDS). *Experimental Review,* 2 (Nov. 1940), 38. (Defunct.)

G4. [First appearance of] A Meditation on Christ's Passion (in TP; all poems in TP were later (Aug. 25, 1946) published in AMITDS; pp. 113-55; see A2; in both volumes poem reads: An Argument: Of the Passion of Christ). *Spirit,* VIII. 2 (May 1941) 44-5.

G5. [First appearance of] Lent in a Year of War (in TP & AMITDS). *View,* 1, 6. (Je. 1941) [a leaf insert between pp. 2 & 3]. (Defunct.)

G6. [First appearance of] The Sponge Full of Vinegar (in TP & AMITDS). *Spirit,* VIII. 3 (Jl. 1941) 80.

---

* A1: Thirty Poems.
A2: A Man in the Divided Sea.
A5: Figures for an Apocalypse.
A12: The Tears of the Blind Lions.
F2: Selected Poems of Thomas Merton.
† *Fordham University Quarterly.* XXIX. 115 (Winter, 1954–1955) [574]-96.
‡ This poem won for the author (Je. 1939), a graduate student of the Faculty of Philosophy, the annual Mariana Griswold van Rensselaer prize for the best example of English lyric verse.

G. The Poetry of Thomas Merton

G7. [First appearance of] The Trappist Abbey: Matins (in TP & AMITDS). *Spirit,* VIII. 4 (Sept. 1941) 111.

G8. [First appearance of] The Flight into Egypt (in TP & AMITDS). *Spirit,* VIII. 5 (Nov. 1941) 148.

G9. [First appearance of] The Night Train, The Dark Morning (in TP & AMITDS); Poem: 1941 (in AMITDS; verse here reads: Poem: 1939), Dirge (in AMITDS). *Poetry,* LX. 1 (Ap. 1942) 20-3.

G10. [First appearance of] Aubade: Lake Erie (in TP & AMITDS). *The New Yorker,* XVIII. 24 (Aug. 1, 1942) 27.

G11. [Second appearance of] The Winter's Night, The Regret (first appearance in TP); [First appearance of] Ash Wednesday, Ariadne, Some Bloody Mutiny, The Greek Women (in AMITDS). *The Quarterly Review of Literature,* 1. 2 (Winter 1944) 76-80.

G12. [Second appearance of] THE SPONGE FULL OF VINEGAR (see G6), THE TRAPPIST ABBEY: MATINS (see G7) (in TP & AMITDS). In Drink From the Rock, Selected Poems from SPIRIT, a Magazine of Poetry, with an Introduction by Helen C. White, Ph.D. New York, The Catholic Poetry Society of America, Incorporated (Ap. 1944); pp. 66, 71.

G13. [First appearance of] Carol (in AMITDS). *The New Yorker,* XX. 45 (Dec. 23, 1944) 36.

G14. [First appearance of] Two States of Prayer (in FFAA). *Voices,* 124 (Winter 1946), 23-4.

G15. [First appearance of] Fugitive, The Ohio River: Louisville, After the Night Office: Gethsemani Abbey (in AMITDS). *Chimera,* IV. 2 (Winter 1946) 2-4. (Defunct.)

G16. [Fourth appearance of] THE TRAPPIST ABBEY: MATINS (See G7, G12) (in TP & AMITDS); [Third appearance of] FOR MY BROTHER (in TP & AMITDS). In A New Anthology of Modern Poetry (Revised Edition), edited, and with an Introduction, by Selden Rodman. New York, The Modern Library (Dec. 1946); pp. 420-1, 422-3. (A Modern Library Giant, #G46.)

G17. [Second appearance of] Two States of Prayer (see G14) (in FFAA); [First appearance of] On the Anniversary of my

[62]

Baptism (in FFAA). *The Commonweal*, XLIII. 26 (Ap. 12, 1946) 640.

G18. [First appearance of] Duns Scotus (in FFAA). *The Commonweal*, XLV. 16 (Jan. 31, 1947) 397.

G19. [First appearance of] A Letter to America (in FFAA). *The Commonweal*, XLV. 17 (Feb. 7, 1947) 419.

G20. [First appearance of] Landscape: Wheatfields (in FFAA). *The Commonweal*, XLV. 19 (Feb. 21, 1947) 463.

G21. [First appearance of] In the Ruins of New York (in FFAA). *The Commonweal*, XLVI. 8 (Je. 6, 1947) 182.

G22. [First appearance of] Canticle for the Blessed Virgin (in FFAA). *The Commonweal*, XLVI. 16 (Aug. 1, 1947) 375.

G23. [First appearance of] Landscape, Prophet and Wild-Dog (in FFAA). *The Western Review*, 12. 1 (Autumn 1947) [30]-1.

G24. [First appearance of] The Landfall (in FFAA). *The Tiger's Eye*, 1. 1 (Oct. 1947) 1-2. (Defunct.)

G25. [Second appearance of] On the Anniversary of my Baptism (see G17) (in FFAA). *The Sewanee Review*, LV. 4 (Oct. 1947; Autumn) [648]-9.

G26. [First appearance of] Natural History (in FFAA). *The Commonweal*, XLVI. 26 (Oct. 10, 1947) 614.

G27. [First appearance of] Theory of Prayer (in FFAA). *The Commonweal*, XLVII. 2 (Oct. 24, 1947) 40.

G28. [First appearance of] Evening: Zero Weather (in FFAA). *Spirit*, XIV. 5 (Nov. 1947) 126-7.

G29. [First appearance of] Clairvaux Prison (in FFAA). *The Catholic Worker*, XIV. 10 (Jan. 1948) 5:1.

G30. [First appearance of] On a Day in August (in TTOTBL). *Epoch*, 1. 2 (Winter 1948) 58-9.

G31. [First appearance of] St. Jerome (in FFAA). *Spirit*, XIV. 6 (Jan. 1948) 159.

G32. [Third appearance of] POEM: 1939 (see A2, G9); [Second appearance of] THE ORACLE, THE BETRAYAL (see A2); [Fifth appearance of] THE SPONGE FULL OF VINEGAR (see A2, G6, G12); [Third appearance of] THE EVENING OF THE VISITATION (see A2) (excerpt: A Man in the Divided Sea). In Return to Tradition (A

G. *The Poetry of Thomas Merton*

Directive Anthology), ed. by Francis B. Thornton, [S.J.]. Milwaukee, The Bruce Publishing Company (Ap. 1948); pp. 851-2.

G33. [First appearance of] The Quickening of St. John the Baptist (in TTOTBL). *Spirit,* XV. 2 (May 1948) 48-50.

G34. [First appearance of] A Psalm (in TTOTBL). *The Commonweal,* XLVIII. 5 (May 14, 1948) 95.

G35. [First appearance of] Messias (not included in his volumes of verse). *Spirit,* XV. 3 (Jl. 1948) 70-1.

G36. [First appearance of] To the Immaculate Virgin on a Winter Night (in TTOTBL). *The Commonweal,* XLVIII. 17 (Aug. 6, 1948) 399.

G37. [First appearance of] Song (in TTOTBL). *Horizon,* XVIII. 105 (Sept. 1948) [153]. (Defunct.)

G38. [First appearance of] Dry Places (in TTOTBL). *The Hudson Review,* 1. 3 (Autumn 1948) [340-1].

G39. [Fourth appearance of] [FOR MY BROTHER: REPORTED MISSING IN ACTION, 1943] (see G16) (in TP & AMITDS) In The Seven Storey Mountain, by Thomas Merton. New York, Harcourt, Brace and Company (Oct. 1948); p. 404.

G40. [First appearance of] From the Legend of St. Clement (in TTOTBL). *The Month,* 1. 1 (Jan. 1949) [5]-6.

G41. [First appearance of] St. Malachy (in TTOTBL); [Second appearance of] From the Legend of St. Clement (see G40) (in TTOTBL). *Poetry,* 73. 5 (Feb. 1949) 255-8.

G42. [First appearance of] A Responsory, 1948 (in TTOTBL). *The Partisan Review,* XVI. 3 (Mar. 1949) 269-70.

G43. [Third appearance of] A LETTER TO AMERICA; LANDSCAPE: WHEATFIELDS (see A5, G19, G20) (excerpt: Figures for an Apocalypse). In the Commonweal Reader, ed. by Edward S. Skillin. New York, Harper & Brothers (Sept. 1949); pp. 288-9, 297-8.

G44. [First appearance of] Like Ilium (not included in his volumes of verse). *Spirit,* XVI. 5 (Nov. 1949) 135.

G45. [First appearance of] Hymn for the Feast of Duns Scotus; Reader (in TTOTBL). *The Atlantic Monthly,* 184. 6 (Dec. 1949) [54-5].

G. The Poetry of Thomas Merton

G46. [Fifth appearance of] FOR MY BROTHER/SGT. JOHN PAUL MERTON, R.C.A.F./REPORTED MISSING IN ACTION, 1943 (see G16, G39) (in TP & AMITDS). In A Second Treasury of the Familiar, ed. by Ralph L. Woods. New York, The Macmillan Company (Ap. 1950); pp. 519-20.

G47. [Third appearance of] EVENING: ZERO WEATHER (see A5, G28); THE QUICKENING OF ST. JOHN THE BAPTIST (see A12, G33); [Second appearance of] MESSIAS (see G35). In From One Word, Selected Poems from "SPIRIT" 1944–1949, ed. by John Gilland Brunini. New York, The Devin-Adair Company (Dec. 1950); pp. 80-1, 96-8, 112-4.

G48. [Sixth appearance of] FOR MY BROTHER:/REPORTED MISSING IN ACTION, 1943 (see G16, G39, G46) (in TP & AMITDS). In Introduction to Poetry, ed. by Mark Van Doren. New York, William Sloane Associates, Incorporated (Feb. 1951); pp. 530-1.

G49. [Seventh appearance of] [FOR MY BROTHER: REPORTED MISSING IN ACTION, 1943] (see G16, G39, G46, G48) (in TP & AMITDS). In The Seven Storey Mountain (Reprint edition; see A7, b), by Thomas Merton. New York, Garden City Books (Feb. 1951); p. 404.

G50. [Eighth appearance of] FOR MY BROTHER:/REPORTED MISSING IN ACTION, 1943 (see G16, G39, G46, G48, G49) (in TP & AMITDS). In Enjoying Poetry, ed. by Mark Van Doren. New York, William Sloane Associates, Incorporated (Jl. 1951); pp. 530-1.

G51. [Second appearance of] A Christmas Card (in FFAA). Perspectives USA/Pilot Issue (Jan. 1952) [192].

G52. [Second appearance of] SPORTS WITHOUT BLOOD/A LETTER TO [the late] DYLAN THOMAS.* In New World Writing/First Mentor Selection (#Ms 73). New York, The New American Library of World Literature Incorporated (Ap. 1952); pp. 74-7.

---

* This poem first appeared in England in 1950 in a volume entitled: Selected Poems of Thomas Merton; see F2. It appears here in an abridged and edited form.

G. *The Poetry of Thomas Merton*

G53. [First appearance of] Early Mass (St. Joseph Infirmary—Louisville) (not included in his volumes of verse). *The Commonweal*, LVI. 2 (Ap. 18, 1952) 48.

G54. [Scattered quotes from the essay:] Poetry and the Contemplative Life [which is included as a supplement to] Figures for an Apocalypse (see A5, B3, C14); [a brief critical piece relative to Merton's poetry;] [an analytical summary of] THE COMMUNION (in TP & AMITDS) [third appearance of this poem which contains four stanzas but here the third stanza is omitted; also mentioned in the discussion but not quoted are the following poems:] TO MY BROTHER REPORTED MISSING IN ACTION, and IN MEMORY OF THE SPANISH POET, LORCA (in TP & AMITDS); [also quoted (third appearance) is the epitaph stanza of] IN THE RUINS OF NEW YORK (see G21) (in FFAA); THE CAPTIVES: A PSALM (in TTOTBL) [second appearance of this poem which contains seven stanzas but here only stanza four, five and seven are quoted;] [a brief analysis of Merton's verse, plus a single line quotation from] DEATH (in TP & AMITDS), [stanza five, line two.] In Modern Poetry and the Christian Tradition (A study in the relation of Christianity to culture), by Amos N. Wilder. New York, Charles Scribner's Sons (Ap. 1952); pp. 13, 114, 115, 141-3, 208, 209.

G55. [Ninth appearance of] [FOR MY BROTHER: REPORTED MISSING IN ACTION, 1943] (see G16, G39, G46, G48, G49, G50) (in TP & AMITDS). In The Seven Storey Mountain (Paper-back edition; see A7, c), by Thomas Merton. [New York,] The New American Library (Ap. 1952); p. 484.

G56. [First appearance of] Christmas, 1951 (For the Carmelites) (not included in his volumes of verse). *The Commonweal*, LVII. 12 (Dec. 26, 1952) 307.

G57. [Fourth appearance of] Poeme: 1939 (see G9, G32) (in AMITDS). *Profils*, 4 (Juillet 1953) 33.

G58. [Second appearance of] LIKE ILIUM (see G44); [Fourth appearance of] TWO STATES OF PRAYER (see G14, G17) (in FFAA); [Second appearance of] ODE TO THE

G. The Poetry of Thomas Merton

PRESENT CENTURY (in AMITDS); [Third appearance of] MESSIAS (see G35, G47). In Joyce Kilmer's Anthology of Catholic Poets, with a new supplement by James Edward Tobin. New York, Image Books (# D15)—A division of Doubleday & Company, Incorporated (Feb. 1955); pp. 321-5.

G59. [Tenth appearance of] "FOR MY BROTHER: REPORTED MISSING IN ACTION, 1943" (see G16, G39, G46, G48, G49, G50, G55) (in TP & AMITDS). In The American Treasury (1455–1955), selected, arranged, and edited by Clifton Fadiman, assisted by Charles Van Doren. New York, Harper & Brothers (Nov. 1955); pp. 616-7. (This poem has five stanzas but here only stanza four and five are quoted.)

G60. [First appearance of] A Prelude: For the Feast of St. Agnes (not included in his volumes of verse). *The Commonweal,* LXIII. 12 (Dec. 23, 1955) 304.

G61. [Second appearance of] Annunciation (original title: Christmas, 1951—For the Carmelites) (see G56); [First appearance of] Stranger (none of these poems are included in his volumes of verse). *The Sign,* 35. 8 (Mar. 1956) 31.

H*

---◆---

TRANSLATIONS INTO FOREIGN

LANGUAGES OF BOOKS, POEMS,

AND ESSAYS

BY

THOMAS MERTON

*ARRANGED ALPHABETICALLY
BY LANGUAGE AND
CHRONOLOGICALLY BY TITLE*

---

* Advisedly I have listed in this section the Merton publications which have appeared in England and Ireland.

H. *Translations of Thomas Merton's Works*

DANISH

H1. DEN STORE STILHED. København, Arne Frost—Hansens Forlag, 1950. A translation, by Kay Nielsen, of The Seven Storey Mountain.

H2. STILHEDENS FORJAETTELSE. København, Arne Frost—Hansens Forlag, 1952. A translation, by Ebba Friis Hansen, of Seeds of Contemplation.

H3. JONASTEGNET. København, Arne Frost—Hansens Forlag, 1955. A translation, by Anna Sofie Scavenius, of The Sign of Jonas.

DUTCH

H4. VAN BALLINGSCHAP EN OVERWINNING. Antwerpen, Sheed & Ward, 1949. A translation, by Jook Steenhoff, of Exile Ends in Glory [contains a new Introduction by Thomas Merton].

H5. DE ROEP DER WONDEN. Antwerpen, Sheed & Ward, 1950. A translation, by Maria Theunen, of What Are These Wounds? [Contains an Introduction by the translator.]

H6. LOUTERINGSBERG. Holland, Het Spectrum, 1950. A translation, by Andre Noorbeek, of The Seven Storey Mountain.

H7. DE WATEREN VAN SILOË. Holland, Het Spectrum, 1950. A translation, by Andre Noorbeek, of The Waters of Siloe.

H8. TER OVERWEGING. Holland, Het Spectrum, 1952. A translation, by Andre Noorbeek, of Seeds of Contemplation.

H9. DE BERG DER WAARHEID. Antwerpen, Sheed & Ward, 1953. A translation, by J. Depres, of The Ascent to Truth.

DUBLIN (IRELAND) PUBLICATIONS

H10. ELECTED SILENCE (The Seven Storey Mountain). Dublin, Clonmore & Reynolds, 1949.

H11. THE WATERS OF SILENCE (The Waters of Siloe). Dublin, Clonmore & Reynolds, 1950.

H12. EXILE ENDS IN GLORY. Dublin, Clonmore & Reynolds, 1951.

H13. WHAT ARE THESE WOUNDS? Dublin, Clonmore & Reynolds, 1952.

LONDON (ENGLAND) PUBLICATIONS

H14. ELECTED SILENCE (The Seven Storey Mountain). London, Hollis & Carter, 1949.

H15. SEEDS OF CONTEMPLATION. London, Hollis & Carter, 1949. [Revised edition published in 1950.]

H16. THE WATERS OF SILENCE (The Waters of Siloe). London, Hollis & Carter, 1950.

H17. WHAT IS CONTEMPLATION? [A pamphlet.] London, Burns Oates & Washbourne, 1950.

H18. THE ASCENT TO TRUTH. London, Hollis & Carter, 1951.

H19. EXILE ENDS IN GLORY. London, Burns Oates & Washbourne, 1951.

H20. WHAT ARE THESE WOUNDS? London, Burns Oates & Washbourne, 1952.

H21. THE SIGN OF JONAS. London, Hollis & Carter, 1953.

H22. BREAD IN THE WILDERNESS. London, Hollis & Carter, 1954.

H23. THE LAST OF THE FATHERS. London, Hollis & Carter, 1955.

H24. NO MAN IS AN ISLAND. London, Hollis & Carter, 1955.

FRENCH

H25. LA NUIT PRIVEE D'ETOILES. Paris, Editions Albin Michel, 1951. A translation, by Marie Tadié, of The Seven Storey Mountain.

H26. SEMENCES DE CONTEMPLATION. Paris, Aux Editions Du Seuil, 1952. A translation, by R. N. Raimbault, of Seeds of Contemplation.

H27. AUX SOURCES DU SILENCE. Paris, Desclée De Brouwer & Cie, 1952. A translation, by Jean Stienon Du Pré, of The Waters of Siloe.

H28. QUELLES SONT CES PLAIES? Paris, Desclée De Brouwer & Cie, 1953. A translation, by a Dominican Nun, of What Are These Wounds? [Contains a Preface by P. Benoit Lavaud, O.P.]

H29. LA MANNE DU DESERT OU LE MYSTERE DES PSAUMES. Paris, Editions De L'Orante, 1954. A translation, by P. Fumaroli, of Bread in the Wilderness.

H30. SAINT BERNARD DE CLAIRVAUX. Paris, Editions D'Histoire Et D'Art, Librairie Plon, 1954. A translation, by Daniel De Maupeou, O.S.B., of The Last of the Fathers.

H31. L'EXIL S'ACHEVE DANS LA GLOIRE. Paris, Desclée De Brouwer & Cie, 1955. A translation, by a Carmelite Nun, of Exile Ends in Glory [with a Preface by M. Gabriel Sortais, and a new Introduction by Thomas Merton].

H32. LE SIGNE DE JONAS. Paris, Editions Albin Michel, 1955. A translation, by Marie Tadié, of The Sign of Jonas.

H33. NUL N'EST UNE ILE. Paris, Aux Editions Du Seuil, 1956. A translation, by Marie Tadié, of No Man Is An Island.

GERMAN

H34. DER BERG DER SIEBEN STUFEN. Zurich, Benziger Verlag, 1950. A translation, by Hans Grossrieder, of The Seven Storey Mountain.

H35. VERHEISSUNGEN DER STILLE. Luzern, Raber-Verlag, 1951. A translation, by Magda Larsen, of Seeds of Contemplation.

H36. DER AUFSTIEG ZUR WAHRHEIT. Zurich, Benziger Verlag, 1952. A translation, by Hans Grossrieder, of The Ascent to Truth.

H37. VON DER VERBANNUNG ZUR HERRLICHKEIT. Luzern, Rex-Verlag, 1953. A translation, by Irene Marinoff, of Exile Ends in Glory.

H38. AUSERWAHLT ZU LEID UND WONNE. Luzern, Raber-Verlag, 1953. A translation, by Pater Sales Hess, of What Are These Wounds? [Contains a Preface by the translator, and an Introduction by Dr. Leddegar Hunkeler.]

H39. DAS ZEICHEN DES JONAS. Zurich, Benziger Verlag, 1954. A translation, by Annemarie Von Puttkamer, of The Sign of Jonas.

H40. BROT IN DER WUSTE. Zurich, Benziger Verlag, 1955. A translation, by Annemarie Von Puttkamer, of Bread in the Wilderness.

H41. KEINER IST EINE INSEL. Zurich, Benziger Verlag, 1956. A translation, by Annemarie Von Puttkamer, of No Man Is An Island.

ITALIAN

H42. LA MONTAGNA DALLE SETTE BALZE. Milano, Garzanti, 1950. A translation, by Alberto Castelli, of The Seven Storey Mountain.

H43. POESIE [a pamphlet; a collection of poems]. Brescia, Morcelliana, 1950. Translator: Augusto Guidi. [The verses assembled here are: La fuga in Egitto, La Vite, La sera della Visitazione, Sera, Il Santissimo sull'altare, Le donne greche, La processione della Candelora, Cana, Trappisti al lavoro, Invocazione a Santa Lucia, S. Tommaso d'Aquino, La biografia, Canto per il Santissimo Sacramento, Chiaravalle.]

H44. LA POESIA E LA VITA CONTEMPLATIVA [a pamphlet]. Brescia, Morcelliana, 1950. A translation, by Augusto Guidi, of the Essay: Poetry and the Contemplative Life; see A5, B3, C14.

H45. SEMI DI CONTEMPLAZIONE. Milano, Garzanti, 1951. A translation, by Bruno Tasso, of Seeds of Contemplation.

H46. LE ACQUE DI SILOE. Milano, Garzanti, 1951. A translation, by Bruno Tasso, of The Waters of Siloe.

H47. CHE COSA E LA CONTEMPLAZIONE [a pamphlet]. Brescia, Morcelliana, 1951. A translation, by Maddalena De Luca, of What Is Contemplation?

H48. CHE SONO QUESTE FERITE? Milano, Garzanti, 1952. A translation, by Cecilia Tirone, of What Are These Wounds?

H49. L'ESILIO E LA GLORIA. Brescia, Morcelliana, 1952. A translation, by P. Giorgia Tansini, of Exile Ends in Glory [contains an Introduction by the translator].

H50. IL SEGNO DI GIONA. Milano, Garzanti, 1953. A translation, by P. Silvio Zarattini, S.J., of The Sign of Jonas.

H51. UN'EQUILIBRATA VITA DI PREGHIERA [a pamphlet]. Brescia, Morcelliana, 1953. A translation, by Maddalena De Luca, of A Balanced Life of Prayer.

H52. ASCESA ALLA VERITA. Milano, Garzanti, 1955. A translation, by Cecilia Tirone, of The Ascent to Truth [contains a Preface by P. Arcadio Larraona, C.M.F.].

H. *Translations of Thomas Merton's Works*

PORTUGUESE

H53. A MONTANHA DOS SETE PATAMARES. Rio De Janeiro, Editora Merito, 1952. A translation, by Jose Geraldo Vieira, of The Seven Storey Mountain.

H54. O SIGNO DE JONAS. Rio De Janeiro, Editora Merito, 1954. A translation, by Jose Geraldo Vieira, of The Sign of Jonas.

H55. SEMENTES DE CONTEMPLACAO. Porto, Livraria Tavares Martins, 1955. A translation, by Teresa Leitao De Barros, of Seeds of Contemplation.

SPANISH

H56. LA MONTANA DE LOS SIETE CIRCULOS. Buenos Aires, Editorial Sudamericana, 1950. A translation, by Aquilino Tur, of The Seven Storey Mountain.

H57. SEMILLAS DE CONTEMPLACION. Buenos Aires, Editorial Sudamericana, 1952. A translation, by C. A. Jordana, of Seeds of Contemplation.

H58. LAS AGUAS DE SILOE. Buenos Aires, Editorial Sudamericana, 1952. A translation, by Maria De Los Dolores Amores Jimenez, of The Waters of Siloe.

II59. VEINTE POEMAS [a pamphlet; a collection of poems]. Madrid, Ediciones Rialp, 1953. Translated and with an Introduction by Jose Maria Valverde.

H60. ASCENSO A LA VERDAD. Buenos Aires, Editorial Sudamericana, 1954. A translation, by Alberto Luis Bixio, of The Ascent to Truth.

H61. EL SIGNO DE JONAS. Mexico, Editorial Cumbre, 1954. A translation, by Julio Fernandez Yanez, of The Sign of Jonas.

H62. LA SENDA DE LA CONTEMPLACION [a pamphlet; a collection of essays]. Madrid, Ediciones Rialp, 1955. A translation, by Antonio Ugalde Y Mariano Del Pozo, of La Renuncia Y El Cristiano (see C44), Una Vida De Oracion Equilibrada (see A14), Que Es La Contemplacion? (see A8, H17, H47), Poesia Y Vida Contemplativa (see A5, B3, C14, H44).

H63. PAN EN EL DESIERTO. Buenos Aires, Editorial Sudamericana,

1955. A translation, by Gonzalo Meneses Ocon, of Bread in
the Wilderness.

H64. SAN BERNARDO, EL ULTIMO DE LOS PADRES. Madrid, Ediciones
Rialp, 1956. A translation, by Father Victorio Peral, of
The Last of the Fathers.

SWEDISH

H65. VAGEN TILL KONTEMPLATION. Stockholm, Petrus De Dacia-
Forlag, 1954. A translation, by Fil Dr. Daniel Andreae, of
Seeds of Contemplation.

I

———— ◆ ————

THE UNPUBLISHED WORKS

OF

THOMAS MERTON

(From 1943 to 1944, while Thomas Merton was a seminarian, he wrote a martyrology of the Cistercian saints. It was never published but it was eventually mimeographed and it is occasionally used by the students. Then from 1950 to 1954, as Master of the Scholastics, he conducted at Our Lady of Gethsemani Abbey a series of spiritual conferences, and the syllabuses of these lectures were later assembled and brought out in eight [mimeographed] volumes for the exclusive use of the seminarians, and copies of those described below are in the Library at Gethsemani.)

I. *Unpublished Works*

11.   CISTERCIAN   1943–1944
STUDIES

CISTERCIAN/STUDIES/BOOK IV/[refers to fourth mimeographed copy]/MODERN/BIOGRAPHICAL SKETCHES/OF/CISTERCIAN/BLESSED AND SAINTS/Edited/by/A Monk of Gethsemani/Abbey of Our Lady of Gethsemani/Trappist, Kentucky/MCMLIV

   1 leaf, i-vii, [1]-26, 1-317 pp. 27¼ x 21½ cm. Bound in red paper with green binding; stapled.

12.   MONASTIC ORIENTATION   1950

MONASTIC ORIENTATION/[Series I]/LECTURES GIVEN TO THE CHOIR NOVICES/ABBEY OF GETHSEMANI/1950

   5 leaves, 1-11, 1-85 pp. 27 x 21 cm. Bound in light blue paper; stapled.

   CONTENTS: (Part I)—The Interior Life—Introduction—Importance of Intellect in Life of Spirit—Studies in the Early Days of the Order—Truth and the Cistercians—Desire-Living by Faith—Life of Grace—Asceticism for Cistercians—Mystical Life and Mystical Prayer—Vocation to the Mystical Life-to Mystical Prayer—Gifts and Virtues—Meditation—Attention—Psychology of Attention—Jesus the Center of Contemplation—The Meaning of the Alleluia—Cistercian Fathers on Prayer—Pentecost and Confirmation—Summary of St. Bernard's Doctrine on the Holy Ghost—Living Faith and "Spiritual Senses"—(Part II)—Monasticism and the Cistercian Spirit—Introduction: "What is a Monk?"—The Testimony of St. John Baptist—Monastic Testimony—Spiritual Virginity I—Spiritual Virginity II—St. Anthony of the Desert—St. Anthony as an Ascete—St. Anthony's Battle Against Temptation—St. Anthony Model of Eremitical Vocation—The Desert Fathers—St. Basil

13.   AN INTRODUCTION TO [1950]
      CISTERCIAN THEOLOGY

AN/INTRODUCTION/TO/CISTERCIAN THEOLOGY/
LECTURES GIVEN TO THE SCHOLASTICS/IN THE CIS-
TERCIAN ABBEY OF GETHSEMANI

5 leaves, 1-79 pp. Bound in grey paper; stapled.
CONTENTS: Preliminary Matter—The Desire of the Soul for
the Knowledge of God—Introduction: The Desire to Know
God—Importance of Knowledge—"scientia Dei"—Scrip-
tural Basis—St Gregory of Nyssa on Moses—Dispositions
in Approach to its Study—Knowledge in Saint Bernard—
Truth in the Cistercian Life—"Curiositas" and "Consider-
atio"—Diagram: St. Benedict's Degrees of Humility and
St. Bernard's Degrees of Truth—Questions for Discussion
(After Sermons 81, 82 In Cantica)—Basis for St. Bernard's
Doctrine on "Image and Likeness" (St. Augustine)—Diagram: Degrees of Ascent to Wisdom—(Part I)—The Region
of Unlikeness (Regio Dissimilitudinis)—Christian Socra-
tism—Need of Recollection to Heal Wounds of "Curiosi-
tas"—Humility—Truth—The Likeness of Jesus—We are
Created to Love God—Portrait of the Soul "in Regione
Dissimilitudinis"—Conversion—The Essence of Conver-
sion—Humility—The Danger of Insensibility—Sidelights on
St. Bernard and Quietism—Abandonment: True and False
—Beatitudes—Self-Will—Consectaria—Trust—"Regio Dis-
similitudinis" in the Monastery—(Part II)—The School of
Charity (Schola Charitatis)—Introduction—Texts: St. Bene-
dict: Prologue—Exordium Magnum—Scriptura—Diagram:
The Sacerdotal Prayer and the Canon of the Mass—Our
Lady and the Nascent Church—Dominici Schola Servitii—
St. Bernard's Pentecost Sermons—Truth as the Basis of
Asceticism—St. Bernard's Epistle to Henry Murdac—St.
Bernard's Dedication Sermons—A Digression on St. Au-
gustine's Enarratio in Ps. 41: (A Source of Cistercian
Teaching on Charity)—Connatural Knowledge of God—

I. *Unpublished Works*

Compassion—Degrees of Love—Union in Penance—Union in Joy

14. MONASTIC ORIENTATION 1951

MONASTIC ORIENTATION/1951/[Series II]/Notes of conferences given to the scholastics at the/Abbey of Gethsemani, during the year 1951.

1 leaf, [1-67], 1-20 pp. 29½ x 23 cm. Bound in blue binder.

15. MONASTIC ORIENTATION 1952

MONASTIC ORIENTATION/SERIES III/(Advent 1951–August 1952)

2 leaves, i-iv, 1-148 pp. Bound in blue paper; stapled.

On recto of leaf 2: These are the notes of the regular/weekly conferences given in the/scholasticate of the Abbey of/Gethsemani, Kentucky/PRO MANUSCRIPTO

CONTENTS: (Part I)—The "Sacrament of Advent" in the Spirituality of St. Bernard—(Part II)—The Spirituality of the First Cistercians—(Part III)—St. Bernard's Lenten Sermons—(Part IV)—St. Bernard—Sermons 49 and 50 "In Cantica"—(Part V)—The Mariale of Adam of Perseigne—(Part VI)—St. Bernard—De Praecepto Et Dispensatione—(Part VII)—Miscellaneous Conferences

16. ACTION AND [1952] CONTEMPLATION

THE SCHOLASTICATE/Abbey of Gethsemani. Texts from the Cistercian Fathers./n.4./ACTION AND CONTEMPLATION—in St. Bernard.

[12] pp (mimeographed). 27½ x 22 cm. Unbound; stapled.

Detailed analyses of a number of sermons pertaining to Saint Bernard (a work-sheet, refers to the three-part article in *Collectanea* of the same name; see C61).

1. Unpublished Works

17. ST. BERNARD ON CONTEMPLATION [1952]

THE SCHOLASTICATE./Abbey of Gethsemani./Texts from the Cistercian Fathers—n.5./ST BERNARD ON CONTEMPLATION.

Single sheet (mimeographed). 27½ x 22 cm.
A brief discourse outlining the basis of "repose" of contemplation.

18. MONASTIC ORIENTATION 1953

MONASTIC ORIENTATION/SERIES IV/(September 1952–November 1953)

1 leaf, i-iv, 1 leaf, 1-151 pp. 27 x 21 cm. Bound in green paper; stapled.
CONTENTS: [Preface]—(Part I)—Aspects of Perfection—Christian Moderation and Temperance—(Part II)—"Quies Monastica"—(Part III)—Introduction to St. Bernard—(Part IV)—Miscellaneous Conferences—(Part V)—Random Notes

19. MONASTIC ORIENTATION* 1954

MONASTIC ORIENTATION/SERIES V/(1953—Advent—1954)/MARIAN YEAR

1 leaf, [i]-iv, 1-152 pp. Bound in orange paper; stapled.
CONTENTS: (Part I)—Mary—Our Marian Year Conferences on Our Lady—especially Her Place in Monastic Spirituality—(Part II)—St. Thomas on "Affability"—(Part III)—Monastic Work—(Part IV)—Miscellaneous Conferences—(Part V)—Priestly Models

---

* Series VI & VII to be mimeographed late in 1956.

I. *Unpublished Works*

I10. SANCTITY IN THE EPISTLES 1954 OF ST. PAUL

SANCTITY/IN THE/EPISTLES OF ST. PAUL/SCRIPTURE COURSE/by/Father M. Louis, O.C.S.O./[quotation in one line]/ Our Lady of GETHSEMANI Abbey/Trappist–Kentucky/1954

2 leaves, [i]-iv, 1-85, 1-26 pp. 27½ x 22 cm. Unbound; not stapled.

CONTENTS: (First Half) (Part I)—The Term "saints"—(Part II)—Sanctity of the Individual and Sanctity of the Community—(Part III)—St. Paul's Conversion—(Part IV)—The Basic Ideas in St. Paul—(Part V)—The Expression "In Christ"—(Part VI)—Recapitulation in Christ—(Part VII)—The Mystery—(Part VIII)—The Eschatology of St. Paul—(Part IX)—The Transfiguration of Man and of Creation—(Part X)—Orientation of the whole Christian life, in hope, to the Parousia—(Part XI)—The Resurrection of the Dead —(Part XII)—The Parousia and the Last Judgment—(Part XIII)—The New Creation—(Second Half) (Part I)—Proemium—Differences between moral and ascetic sections—(Part II)—Baptism and Faith—(Part III)—Human nature in St. Paul (his psychology)—(Part IV)—Flesh and Spirit in St. Paul

I11. SCRIPTURE EXAM 1954

SCRIPTURE EXAM/1954/"SANCTITY IN THE EPISTLES OF ST. PAUL"

Single sheet (mimeographed); sky blue. 35¼ x 21½ cm.
Four questions based upon "Sanctity in the Epistles of St. Paul"; see I10.

I. *Unpublished Works*

112.   NOTES ON SACRED ART   1954

NOTES ON SACRED ART/Conferences given to the Scholastics/Abbey of Gethsemani, Kentucky/October and November 1954

2 leaves, [1]-30 pp. 28 x 22 cm. Bound in cream paper; stapled.

CONTENTS: Preamble: What is Sacred Art?—(Part I: Some Thoughts on Sacred Art)—Importance of Sacred Art—Definition—Art in the Middle Ages, Renaissance, Modern Times—(Part II: The "Sacred" in Art)—"Sacred" vs "Academic" Art—The Marks of Sacred Art—(Part III: Tradition and Convention)—(Part IV: Instruction of the Holy Office)—Norms in Architecture and Art—Real Traditionalism—(Part V: Eric Gill on Art)—Sacred and Secular Viewpoints in Art and Work—Solution and Critique—(Part VI: The Cistercians and Sacred Art)—Cluny and Revival of Romanesque Art—Justification of Attitude of Cluny—Commentary—Art of Cluny in Social and Spiritual Context—Saint Bernard and the Cistercians on Art—The Apologia—Spirit and Outline of Tract—Analysis—Section on Church Art (Chapter XII)—Art and the First Cistercians—Conclusion and Summary—Building a Cistercian Monastery—Logic of Cistercian Monastery Planning—Plan: A Twelfth Century Monastery—Plan: A Modern Monastery

113.   BASIC PRINCIPLES OF   1955
MONASTIC SPIRITUALITY

BASIC/PRINCIPLES/of/MONASTIC SPIRITUALITY/by/ Father M. Louis, O.C.S.O./[quotation in one line]/Our Lady of Gethsemani/Trappist—1955—Kentucky.

2 leaves, [1]-18 pp (mimeographed). 27½ x 22 cm. Unbound; stapled.

CONTENTS: Quem Quaeritis?—Verbum Caro Factum Est—Verbum Crucis—Children of the Resurrection—Filii Et Haeredes Dei—Sponsa Christi—Conclusion

I. *Unpublished Works*

SPECIAL ITEMS

The listing that follows will include a prayer card, sermons, a spiritual conference, a dust-wrapper portrait, a leaflet, a preface, and a post-card which were authored by Thomas Merton.

114. MOTHER M. BERCHMANS PIGUET, O.C.S.O. 1876–1915

(N.p., n.d.) [1947]
Prayer-Card. 12 x 8 cm.
This brief biography and prayer was written to accompany the prayer-card photographic reproduction, in brown and white, of Mother Berchmans which appears on the recto.

115. SERMON FOR DEDICATION OF CHURCH—1951

(final version)

Single sheet (yellow carbon sheet). 27½ x 22 cm.
The text of this sermon is taken from Baruch: 6:6: "For my angel is with you and will watch over your soul."

116. THE MONASTIC LIFE—1952

Seven sheets (white carbon sheets). 27½ x 22 cm.
A spiritual conference which deals with the monastic life. It explains that such a life "is a search for God", an "adoration of God" and the "life radiates God."

I17. A PORTRAIT OF SAINT CATHERINE OF SIENA

This painting, which Merton completed in 1952, was for book-jacket of Sigrid Undset's "KATHARINA BENINCASA." It was published in Germany by Bonner Buchgemeinde in 1953.

I18. PRIESTLY DAY OF PRAYER

Leaflet, [1-4] pp. 12½ x 7½ cm. Abbey of Gethsemani, Trappist, Kentucky, 1954.

A short meditation and litany on the Canticle of Canticles printed on pale blue paper.

I19. EPIPHANY SERMON—1955

Single sheet (white carbon sheet). 27½ x 22 cm.

The text of this sermon is taken from John: 1: "We have seen His glory, the glory as of the only-begotten Son of the Father, full of grace and truth—and of His fulness we have all received."

I20. A PREFACE—Feb. 11, 1955

Three sheets (white carbon sheets). 27½ x 22 cm.

This was written for the English translation of Pere Francois De Ste Marie's "PRESENCE A DIEU ET A SOI-MEME." The volume has not been published as of this writing.

I21. O, COME, O HASTEN . . .

Post-Card. 13½ x 9½ cm. Impressor: Casa Vallelle, Rio De Janeiro, Brasil [1955].

This official hymn of the XXXVI International Eucharistic

I. *Unpublished Works*

Congress, which is in seven stanzas of four lines each with Christian symbols stamped in red and gold alongside each stanza, was written by D. Marcos Barbosa, O.S.B., and translated by Thomas Merton.

J

———— ◆ ————

JUVENILIA

CONTRIBUTIONS BY

THOMAS MERTON

TO SCHOOL PUBLICATIONS

The following abbreviations are used: CJ (The
Columbia Jester); CR (The Columbia Review), and CS
(The Columbia Spectator).

ARRANGED CHRONOLOGICALLY

J. Juvenilia

J1. Editorial; An Unfortunate Oakhamian [black and white cartoon drawn by author accompanies article]; Motlie Notis [minus the poem, which was by someone else]; The City Without a Soul [title and some of the remarks were dictated by the Moderator of the Magazine!]. *The Oakhamian*, XLVII (Christmas Term—1931) [1], 18, 19, 23-4.

J2. Editorial; Society Notes; Strasbourg Cathedral; The New Boy Who Won Through; Lines to a Crafty Septuagenarian [a poem]; On the Musical Propensities of VI Classical [a poem]; Answers to Correspondents. *The Oakhamian*, XLVII (Easter Term—1932) [1], 16-8, 18, 21-2, 24, 27, 28.

J3. Editorial; Dies Orationum [a poem]; Wahlt Hitler. *The Oakhamian*, XLVII (Summer Term—1932) [1], 25, 29-30.

J4. Editorial; The Passing of Sir Lafournayse; Fragment of Roman Bas-relief [black and white cartoon drawn by author accompanies article]; Certificate Y; A Classical Ditty [a poem]. *The Oakhamian*, XLVIII (Christmas Term—1932) [1], 22, 23, 25-6, 26.

J5. Paris in Chicago. *The Granta*, XLIII. 971 (Nov. 29, 1933) 144.

J6. A Crust for Egoists. *The Granta*, XLIII. 981 (Ap. 25, 1934) 355.

J7. [A letter to] *Esquire*, II. 6 (Nov. 1934) 14.

J8. Katabolism of an Englishman. *CJ*, XXVI. 1 (Sept. 1935) 12, plus 28.

J9. Suburban Demon. *CJ*, XXVI. 3 (Nov. 1935) 7.

J10. At the Corner. *CR*, XVII. 1 (Nov. 1935) 8.

J11. The More Abundant Life; Students Awake. *CJ*, XXVI. 4 (Dec. 1935) 14, 15, plus 39.

J12. The Chaste. *CJ*, XXVI. 5 (Jan. 1936) 18, plus 22.

J13. Springtime for Webster. *CJ*, XXVI. 6 (Feb. 1936) 15.

J14. Success Story. *CJ*, XXVI. 7 (Mar. 1936) 12, plus 33.

J15. Chorines vs. Ponies: Who Wins? *CS*, LIX. 100 (Mar. 18, 1936) 1:3.

J16. Bob Burke Loses Jinx Fight on Technical K. O. in Garden. *CS*, LIX. 104 (Mar. 24, 1936) 1:2, plus 3:2.

J. *Juvenilia*

J17. Burke's Shoulder Old-Time Jinx. *CS*, LIX. 105 (Mar. 25, 1936) 3:5.

J18. Spring Gets Jester Editors; Boys Plan Barnard Section. *CS*, LIX. 114 (Ap. 7, 1936) 1:2.

J19. [A column; The Off-Hour.] *CS*, LIX. 118 (Ap. 16, 1936) 2:2.

J20. [A column; The Stroller.] *CS*, LIX. 124 (Ap. 24, 1936) 2:2.

J21. Napoleon or Something. *CJ*, XXVI. 9 (May 1936) 11-2.

J22. [A column; The Off-Hour.] *CS*, LIX. 130 (May 4, 1936) 2:2.

J23. [A column; The Stroller.] *CS*, LIX. 135 (May 11, 1936) 2:3.

J24. They Grow in September; The Best Things in Life; Your Night to Howl. *CJ*, XXXVII. 1 (Sept. 1936) 12, 14, 16-9.

J25. [An untitled story about the Observation Roofs which was included in the column:] "WHAT GOES ON". *Rockefeller Center Weekly*, 5. 10 (Sept. 4, 1936) 13. (Defunct.)

J26. Did the Reds Get Evander Crotch? *CJ*, XXXVII. 2 (Oct. 1936) 28-31.

J27. [A column; The Stroller.] *CS*, LX. 17 (Oct. 16, 1936) 2:2.

J28. Latins are Lousy Pornographers; Concerning Tennyson McGap. *CJ*, XXXVII. 3 (Nov. 1936) 14-5, 18.

J29. How Time Goes; Your Night to Howl. *CJ*, XXXVIII. 4 (Dec. 1936) 26-7, 32-3.

J30. [A column; The Stroller.] *CS*, LX. 91 (Mar. 11, 1937) 2:2.

J31. Raw Lie Unraw [first line of untitled poem]. *CJ*, XXXIX. 2 (Oct. 1937) 16.

J32. Mr. and Mrs. Jim Huttner. *CR*, XIX. 1 (Nov. 1937) 8-13.

J33. Nineteen Questions for Social Blights. *CJ*, XXXIX. 3 (Nov. 1937) 24.

J34. Happy Planets, Happy Beasts [a poem]. *CJ*, XXXIX. 4 (Dec. 1937) 16.

J35. Old Glory, Old Junk. *CJ*, XXXIX. 5 (Jan. 1938) 8, plus 23.

J36. Window [a poem]; Voyage to Nyack; Your Night to Howl. *CJ*, XXXIX. 7 (Mar. 1938) 10, 12, plus 26, 21.

J37. Huxley and the Ethics of Peace. *CR*, XIX. 2 (Mar. 1938) 13-8.

J38. Look, Tiger; Spring for All [poems]. *CJ*, XXXIX. 8 (Ap. 1938) 33.

J39. Bureaucrats: Diggers [a poem]. *CR*, XIX. 3 (Summer 1938)

J. Juvenilia

13. (This poem is included in Columbia Poetry; see G1.)

J40. Anatomy of Journals. *CJ*, XXXIX. 9 (May 1938) 10, plus 28.

J41. Fourth Discourse Concerning the Elephant; Pastoral for Maytime [a poem]; Legends are all Lies. *CJ*, XXXIX. 10 (Je. 1938) 7, 14, 18-9.

J42. Oasis: A Crust for the Frosh. *CJ*, XL. 1 (Sept. 1938) 21, plus 29.

J43. Oasis: M. A. Thesis; Woods are not Sober [first line of untitled poem]. *CJ*, XL. 2 (Oct. 1938) 16, 24.

J44. High Life: Sleep; Martians. *CJ*, XL. 3 (Nov. 1938) 10-1, 13.

J45. Two Things for Christmas [a poem]; [A review of] Garland of Bays, by Gwyn Jones. *CJ*, XL. 4 (Dec. 1938) 14, 27.

J46. Fable of Heriger. *CJ*, XL. 6 (Feb. 1939) 11.

J47. Concerning Tennyson McGap. *CJ*, XL. 9 (May 1939) 7.

J48. The Question of the Beard. *CJ*, C. 1 (Sept. 1939) 10-1.

J49. Masque of Melancholy. *CJ*, C. 2 (Oct. 1939) 20-1.

J50. The Art of Richard Hughes. *CR*, XXI. 1 (Nov. 1939) 13-8.

J51. Fable: The Profiteer, by F. Xavier Sheridan [Merton's nom de plume]. *CJ*, C. 4 (Dec. 1939) 6-7.

J52. The Beetle Becomes the Prince of Creatures and Makes a Choice (an opera), by F. X. Sheridan [to my knowledge, these are the only two instances where Father Louis has used a pseudonym]. *CJ*, C. 8 (Ap. 1940) 24-6.

INDEX

BOOK INDEX

INDEX OF MERTON ARTICLES

INDEX OF ARTICLES ABOUT
  MERTON

POETRY INDEX

INDEX OF FOREIGN PUBLICATIONS

INDEX OF TRANSLATORS

INDEX OF UNPUBLISHED ITEMS,
  ETC.

INDEX OF JUVENILIA

INDEX OF NAMES

BOOK INDEX

American Treasury, The, B19, G59
Ascent to Truth, The, A15

Balanced Life of Prayer, A, A14
Bernard, St., of Clairvaux, B14
Bread in the Wilderness, A18
Burning Oracle, The, C10
Burnt Out Incense, B2

Catholic Bedside Book, The, B16
Catholic Digest Reader, The, B10
Christian Conversation, B11
Cistercian Contemplatives, A4
City of God, The, B4
Columbia Poetry, G1
Commonweal Reader, The, B3, G43
Commonweal Treasury, The, B20
Consolations of Catholicism, The, B17
Convertis Du XXᵉ Siecle, D65

Defense of Art, C4
Devotions in Honor of Saint John of
  the Cross, A16
Drink From the Rock, G12

Enjoying Poetry, G50
Enjoyment of Literature, The, C3
Exile Ends in Glory, A6

Figures for an Apocalypse, A5
From an Abundant Spring, D50
From One Word, G47

Garland of Bays, J45
Gethsemani Magnificat, A10
Guide to Cistercian Life, A3

Happy Crusaders, The, B8

I Sing of a Maiden, C20
Introduction to Poetry, G48

Joyce Kilmer's Anthology of Catholic
  Poets, G58

Kingdom of Jesus, The, E1

Last of the Fathers, The, A19
Laughter in the Dark, C2
La Vie Eremitique, B21
Lawrence, D. H., and Susan his Cow,
  C11
Living Bread, The, A21

Man in the Divided Sea, A, A2
Modern Poetry and the Christian
  Tradition, G54

National Catholic Almanac, The, B15
New Anthology of Modern Poetry, A,
  B1, G16
New Treasure Chest, The, B13
New World Writing, G52
No Man Is An Island, A20

Personal Heresy, The, C8
Perspectivas Dos Estados Unidos, B18
Pillar of Fire, The, B7
Plato Today, C6

Religious Trends in English Poetry,
  C9
Return to Tradition, D12, G32
Romanticism and the Gothic Revival,
  C5

Saints for Now, B9
Second Treasury of the Familiar, A,
  G46
Seeds of Contemplation, A9
Selected Poems of Thomas Merton, F2
Seven Storey Mountain, The, A7, G39,
  G49, G55
Sign of Jonas, The, A17
Silence dans le Ciel, B22
Skelton, John, Laureate, C7
Soul of the Apostolate, The, E2
Spirit of Simplicity, The, E3

Tears of the Blind Lions, The, A12
Third Spiritual Alphabet, The, C23
Thirty Poems, A1

[97]

Book Index

Treasury of Catholic Thinking, A, B12

Waters of Silence, The, F1
Waters of Siloe, The, A11

We Speak for Ourselves, B6
What Are These Wounds?, A13
What Is Contemplation?, A8
Where I Found Christ, B5
World's Body, The, C1

INDEX OF MERTON ARTICLES

Active and Contemplative Orders, C18
Art Speaks to a Soul, B17
Ascent to Truth, The, C58
August Seventh, B11

Bernard of Clairvaux, C74
Bernard, St., Action and Contemplation in, C79
Bernard, St., Et L'Amerique, C72
Bernard, St., Le Sacrement De L'Avent Dans La Spiritualite De, C62
Bernard, St., Monk and Apostle, C66, C75
Bread in the Wilderness, C78
Brief Comment, A, B7
Brief Comment, A, on Religious Poetry, B1

Cause of our Joy, The, C24
Christ Suffers Again, C60
Christmas Devotion, A, C19
Christmas Sermons of Bl. Guerric, The, C95
Contemplation in a Rocking Chair, C25
Contemplative Life can be Led by All, The, B12
Contemplative Life, The, C40

Dans Le Desert De Dieu, C83
Death of a Trappist, C16, C21
Der Heilige Johannes Vom Kreuz, C71

Elected Silence, C33
Etapes De Mon Chemin Vers Dieu, C57

First Christmas at Gethsemani, C41
Foreword, B2
Foreword, A, B14

Gift of Understanding, The, C31
Grace at Work, C29

How to Believe in God, C59
Huxley's Pantheon, C12

I Begin to Meditate, B10, C30, C32
I Will be Your Monk, C49
In Silentio, B22
Introduction, An, B4
Invisible Seeds, B13
Is Mysticism Normal?, C38

John, St., of the Cross, B9, C68, C69

Le Moine Et Le Chasseur, C53
Le Recueillement, C90
Les Psaumes Et La Contemplation, C65

Merton, Thomas, Book Reviews by, C1, C2, C3, C4, C5, C6, C7, C8, C9, C10, C11, C20, C23
Merton, Thomas, Denies Rumors, C54
Merton, Thomas, O Diario De, C77
Merton Thomas, On Renunciation, C52
Monks and Hunters, C55
Mystical Verse, C13

N.D. Gethsemani, Annual Report, C48, C56, C61, C80, C86
Nel Deserto, C81
No Man Is An Island, C84, C88, C89, C91

O Ultimo Padre Da Igreja, B18
One Sunday in New York, C28
One's Own Virtues, B13

Peace That is War, C36
Poetry and the Contemplative Life, A5, B3, C14
Poverty, C34
Praying the Psalms, C93
Preface, B21
Primacy of Contemplation, The, C45
Primary Apostolate, The, B15
Psalms and Contemplation, The, C51
Psalms as Poetry, The, C76

Raccoglimento, C92
Reality, Art, and Prayer, C82

[99]

San Giovanni Della Croce, C70
Schoolboy in England, C26
Schoolboy's Lament, C35
Seeds of Contemplation, B8, B19, C67, C73
Self-Denial and the Christian, C44
September, 1949, C43
Sign of Jonas, The, C64
Something to Live For, C87
Student, Man-About-The-Campus, Atheist, Trappist Monk, B6
Sweet Savor of Liberty, The, C27

Todo y Nada, C46
Tower of Babel, The, C94
Transforming Union in Saints Ber-
nard and John of the Cross, The, C42
Trappist Speaks on People, Priests and Prayer, A, C22
Trappists go to Utah, The, B3, B20, C15, C17
Trappists Make Silent Martyrs, C39
Truly a Success as a Cistercian, B16

Un Americano A Roma, C47

Waters of Siloe, The, C37
White Pebble, The, B5, C50

You and I, C85

INDEX OF ARTICLES
ABOUT MERTON

Action and Contemplation, D27
Ascent to Truth, The, D47

Belly of a Paradox, In the, D54
Benedictine versus Trappist, D52
Bernard, St., Action and Contemplation in, D70

Catholic Author of the Month, D23
Christmas Meditation, A, D9
Cistercians, The, D32
Commentary Note on the Merton Problem, A, D40
Complete Twentieth-Century Man, The, D19

Elected Silence, D25, D29
Everyman's Vocation, D49
Exciting Autobiography Condemns Modernism, D16

Flash of Dark Lightning, D67
From the Belly of the Whale, D55
Fruits of Mysticism, The, D26

If you are Looking, Look inside Yourself, D46

Journey to Gethsemani, A, D74

La Tua Solitudine Portera Frutti Immensi, D41
Le Cardinal Et Le Trappists, D48
Le Pain Des Psaumes, D66
Letter, A, D31

Malachy, St., D18
Merton, Thomas, D12
Merton, Thomas, A Bibliography of, D68
Merton, Thomas, A Modern Man in Reverse, D51

Merton, Thomas, And Dom Aelred Graham, D59
Merton, Thomas, And his Critics, D64
Merton, Thomas, And the Critics, D38
Merton, Thomas, And T. S. Eliot, D69
Merton, Thomas, As a Poet, Form and Content, D44
Merton, Thomas, Der Fall, D34
Merton, Thomas, His Problem and a Solution, D24
Merton, Thomas, His Word and his Spirit, D11
Merton, Thomas, In Defense of, D57
Merton's, Thomas, Jonas, D62
Merton, Thomas, La Conversion Et L'Ordination De, D35
Merton's, Thomas, Most Recent Poems, D33
Merton, Thomas, O Diario De, D63
Merton, Thomas, On the Monastic Life, D60
Merton, Thomas, Poet, D7
Merton, Thomas, Poet of Contemplation, D39
Merton, Thomas, Poet of the Contemplative Life, D21
Merton, Thomas, Poeta Della Contemplazione, D42
Merton, Thomas, Poete Et Trappiste, D65
Merton, Thomas, The Meaning of, D53
Merton, Thomas, The Mysticism of, D73
Merton, Thomas, The Poetry of, D50
Merton, Thomas, The Verses of, D1
Merton, Thomas, Trappist, D28
Modern or Medievalist?, D4
Moisson De Silence, D43
Mountain, The, D20
Mystics Among Us, D14

Articles About Merton

New Directions Presents a Catholic
Poet, D2
No Man Is An Island, D72
Notes and Meditations, D71

O Diario Sem Tempo, D61

Poet of Genuine Talent, A, D5
Poet Turned Monk, The, D3
Poetry and Contemplation, D8
Poetry in Education, D45
Prophecy for the Atomic Age, D13

Seven Storey Mountain, The, D15
Sign of Jonas, The, D58
Something of a Monk's Spiritual Life,
D56

Toast of the Avant-Garde, D10
Trappist Canticle, A, D6
Trappist Monastery, D22
Two Letters on the Merton Problem,
D36, D37

Waters of Siloe, The, D30
White Man's Culture, D17

POETRY INDEX

Advent, A2
(Advice to my Friends Robert Lax and
Edward Rice, to get away while they
still can.) A5
After the Night Office: Gethsemani,
A2, G15
Agnes, St., A Prelude: For the Feast
of, G60
Agnes, St., A Responsory, A1, A2
Alberic, St., A2
An Argument: Of the Passion of
Christ, A1, A2, G4
Anniversary of my Baptism, On the,
A5, G17, G25
Annunciation, G61
(Apoc. xiv, 14.) A5
April, A2
Aquinas, St. Thomas, A2
Ariadne, A2, G11
Ariadne at the Labyrinth, A1, A2
Ash Wednesday, A2, G11
Aubade: Bermuda, G1
Aubade: Harlem, A2
Aubade: Lake Erie, A1, A2, G10
Aubade: The Annunciation, A2
Aubade: The City, A2

Baptist, St. John, A2
Betrayal, The, A2, G32
Biography, The, A2
Blessed Virgin Mary Compared to a
Window, The, A1, A2
Bombarded City, The, A2
Bureaucrats: Diggers, G1, J39

Calypso's Island, A2
Cana, A2
Candlemas Procession, The, A2
Canticle for the Blessed Virgin, A5,
G22; Envoi in book only
Captives, The, A Psalm, A12, G54
Carol, A2, G13
Christmas, 1951, G56
Christmas as to People, G1

Christmas Card, A, A5, G51
City After Noon, The, A12
Clairvaux, A2
Clairvaux Prison, A5, G29
Columbus, Christopher, A12
Communion, The, A1, A2, G54
Crusoe, A2

Dark Encounter, The, A2
Dark Morning, The, A1, A2, G9
Day in August, On a, A12, G30
Death, A1, A2, G54
Dirge, A2, G9
Dirge for a Town in France, A2
Dirge for the Proud World, A1, A2
Dreaming Trader, The, A2
Dry Places, A12, G38

Early Mass, G53
Evening, A1, A2
Evening of the Visitation, The, A1,
A2, G32
Evening: Zero Weather, A5, G28, G47

Fable for a War, G1, G2
Fall of Night, The, A2
Figures for an Apocalypse, A5; refers
to a group of eight poems (pp. 13-
28) in aforementioned book
Flight into Egypt, The, A1, A2, G8
For my Brother, A1, A2, G16, G39,
G46, G48, G49, G50, G54, G55, G59
Freedom as Experience, A5
From the Legend of St. Clement, A12,
G40, G41
Fugitive, A2, G15

Greek Women, The, A2, G11

Heavenly City, The, A5
Holy Child's Song, The, A1, A2
Holy Communion: The City, A1, A2
Holy Sacrament of the Altar, The,
A1, A2
House of Caiphas, The, A2

[103]

How Long we Wait, A2
Hymn for the Feast of Duns Scotus, A12, G45

Image of True Lovers' Death, The, A2
Iphigenia: Politics, A1, A2

Jason, St., A1, A2
Je Crois En L'Amour, A12
Jerome, St., A5, G31
John's, St., Night, A5

La Salette, A2
Landfall, The, A5, G24
Landscape: Beast, A5
Landscape, Prophet and Wild-Dog, A5, G23
Landscape: Wheatfields, A5, G20, G43
Lent in a Year of War, A1, A2, G5
Letter to America, A, A5, G19, G43
Letter to my Friends, A2
Like Ilium, G44, G58
Litany, G1
Lucy, St., An Invocation to, A2

Malachy, St., A12, G41
Man in the Wind, The, A2
Meditation on Christ's Passion, A, A1, A2, G4
Memory of the Spanish Poet, In, A1, A2, G54
Messenger, The, A1, A2
Messias, G35, G47, G58
Mysterious Song in the Spring of the Year, A, A5

Natural History, A5, G26
Night Train, The, A1, A2, G9

Ode to the Present Century, A2, G58
Ohio River: Louisville, A2, G15
Oracle, The, A2, G32

Paul, St., A2
Paul, St., the Hermit, A5
Peril, The, A2
Pilgrims' Song, A5

Poem, A1, A2
Poem, 1939, A2, G9, G32, G57
Poem, 1941, A2, G9
Poeme, 1939, A2, G57
Poet, to his Book, The, A5
Pride of the Dead, The, A2
Prophet, A1, A2
Psalm, A, A12, G34

Quickening of St. John the Baptist, The, A12, G33, G47

Rahab's House, A2
Rain and the Sun, In the, A12
Reader, The, A12, G45
Regret, The, A1, A2, G11
Responsory, 1948, A, A12, G42
Rievaulx: St. Ailred, A5
Ruins of New York, In the, A5, G21, G54

Scotus, Duns, A5, G18
Senescente Mundo, A12
Snare, The, A2
Some Bloody Mutiny, A2, G11
Song, A2, G3
Song, A2
Song, A12, G37
Song, A, A2
Song: Contemplation, A5
Song for Our Lady of Cobre, A1, A2
Song for the Blessed Sacrament, A2
Song of the Traveller, The, A5
Sowing of Meanings, The, A5
Sponge Full of Vinegar, The, A1, A2, G6, G12, G32
Sports Without Blood, F2, G52
Spring: Monastery Farm, A5
Storm at Night, The, A2
Stranger, G61

Theory of Prayer, A5, G27
These Years a Winter, G1
Three Postcards from the Monastery, A5
To the Immaculate Virgin Mary, on a Winter Night, A12, G36
Transformation: For the Sacred Heart, A5

Poetry Index

Trappist Abbey: Matins, The, A1, A2, G7, G12, G16

Trappist Cemetery: Gethsemani, The, A2

Trappists: Working, A2

Tropics, A2

Two Desert Fathers, A5

Two States of Prayer, A5, G14, G17, G58

Victory, The, A2

Vine, The, A1, A2

Whitsun Canticle, A, A2; Envoi in book only

Widow of Nain, The, A2

Winter Afternoon, A5

Winter's Night, The, A1, A2, G11

Word, A Responsory, The, A2

INDEX OF FOREIGN PUBLICATIONS

DANISH

Den Store Stilhed, H1
Jonastegnet, H3
Stilhedens Forjaettelse, H2

DUTCH

De Berg Der Waarheid, H9
De Roep Der Wonden, H5
De Wateren Van Siloë, H7
Louteringsberg, H6
Ter Overweging, H8
Van Ballingschap En Overwinning, H4

IRISH

Elected Silence, H10
Exile Ends in Glory, H12
Waters of Silence, The, H11
What Are These Wounds?, H13

ENGLISH

Ascent to Truth, The, H18
Bread in the Wilderness, H22
Elected Silence, H14
Exile Ends in Glory, H19
Last of the Fathers, The, H23
No Man Is An Island, H24
Seeds of Contemplation, H15
Sign of Jonas, The, H21
Waters of Silence, The, H16
What Are These Wounds?, H20
What Is Contemplation?, H17

FRENCH

Aux Sources Du Silence, H27
La Manne Du Desert Ou Le Mystere Des Psaumes, H29
La Nuit Privee D'Etoiles, H25
L'Exil S'Acheve Dans La Gloire, H31
Le Signe De Jonas, H32
Nul N'Est Une Ile, H33
Quelles Sont Ces Plaies?, H28
Saint Bernard De Clairvaux, H30
Semences De Contemplation, H26

GERMAN

Auserwahlt Zu Leid Und Wonne, H38
Brot In Der Wuste, H40
Das Zeichen Des Jonas, H39
Der Aufstieg Zur Wahrheit, H36
Der Berg Der Sieben Stufen, H34

Keiner Ist Eine Insel, H41
Verheissungen Der Stille, H35
Von Der Verbannung Zur Herrlichkeit, H37

ITALIAN

Ascesa Alla Verita, H52
Che Cosa E La Contemplazione?, H47
Che Sono Queste Ferite?, H48
Il Segno Di Giona, H50
La Montagna Dalle Sette Balze, H42
La Poesia E La Vita Contemplativa, H44
Le Acque Di Siloe, H46
L'Esilio E La Gloria, H49
· Poesie, H43
Semi Di Contemplazione, H45
Un'Equilibrata Vita Di Preghiera, H51

PORTUGUESE

A Montanha Dos Sete Patamares, H53
O Signo De Jonas, H54
Sementes De Contemplacao, H55

SPANISH

Ascenso A La Verdad, H60
El Signo De Jonas, H61
La Montana De Los Siete Circulos, H56
La Senda De La Contemplacion, H62
Las Aguas De Siloe, H58
Pan En El Desierto, H63
San Bernardo, El Ultimo De Los Padres, H64
Semillas De Contemplacion, H57
Veinte Poemas, H59

SWEDISH

Vagen Till Kontemplation, H65

INDEX OF TRANSLATORS

Andreae, Fil Dr. Daniel, H65

Bixio, Alberto Luis, H60

Castelli, Alberto, H42

De Barros, Teresa Leitao, H55
De Luca, Maddalena, H47, H51
Del Pozo, Antonio Ugalde Y Mariano, H62
Depres, J., H9
Du Pre, Jean Stienon, H27

Fumaroli, P., H29

Grossrieder, Hans, H34, H36
Guidi, Augusto, H43, H44

Hansen, Ebba Friis, H2
Hess, Pater Sales, H38

Jimenez, Maria De Los Delores Amores, H58
Jordana, C. A., H57

Larsen, Magda, H35

Marinoff, Irene, H37
Maupcou, Daniel De, H30
Monteiro, Adolfo Casais, B18

Nielsen, Kay, H1
Noorbeek, Andre, H6, H7, H8

Ocon, Gonzalo Meneses, H63

Peral, Father Victorio, H64

Raimbault, R. N., H26

Scavenius, Anna Sofie, H3
Steenhoff, Jook, H4

Tadié, Marie, B22, H25, H32, H33
Tansini, P. Giorgia, H49
Tasso, Bruno, H45, H46
Theunen, Maria, H5
Tirone, Cecilia, H48, H52
Tur, Aquilino, H56

Valverde, Jose Maria, H59
Vieira, Jose Geraldo, H53, H54
Von Puttkamer, Annemarie, H39, H40, H41

Yanez, Julio Fernandez, H61

Zarattini, P. Silvio, H50

INDEX OF UNPUBLISHED
ITEMS, ETC.

Action and Contemplation, I6

Basic Principles on Monastic Spirituality, I13
Bernard, St., on Contemplation, I7

Cistercian Studies, I1

Epiphany Sermon, I19

Introduction to Cistercian Theology, An, I3

Monastic Life, The, I16
Monastic Orientation, I2, I4, I5, I8, I9

Notes on Sacred Art, I12

O, Come, O Hasten, I21

Paul, St., Sanctity in the Epistles of, I10
Piguet, Mother M. Berchmans, I14
Portrait of Saint Catherine of Siena, A, I17
Preface, A, I20
Priestly Day of Prayer, I18

Scripture Exam, I11
Sermon for Dedication of Church, I15

INDEX OF JUVENILIA

Anatomy of Journals, J40
Answers to Correspondents, J2
At the Corner, J10

Best Things in Life, The, J24
Bob Burke Loses Jinx Fight, J16
Book Review, J45
Boys Plan Barnard Section, J18
Bureaucrats: Diggers, J39
Burke's Shoulder Old-Time Jinx, J17

Certificate Y, J4
Chaste, The, J12
Chorines vs Ponies, J15
City Without a Soul, The, J1
Classical Ditty, A, J4
Column, J19, J20, J22, J23, J27, J30
Concerning Tennyson McGap, J28,
    J47
Crust for Egoists, A, J6
Crust for the Frosh, A, J42

Did the Reds get Evander Crotch?,
    J26
Dies Orationum, J3

Editorial, J1, J2, J3, J4

Fable of Heriger, J46
Fable: The Profiteer, J51
Fourth Discourse Concerning the Ele-
    phant, J41
Fragment of Roman Bas-relief, J4

Happy Planets, Happy Beasts, J34
High Life: Sleep, J44
How Time Goes, J29
Hughes, Richard, The Art of, J50
Huxley and the Ethics of Peace, J37

Katabolism of an Englishman, J8

Latins are Lousy Pornographers, J28
Legends are all Lies, J41

Letter, A, J7
Lines to a Crafty Septuagenarian, J2
Look, Tiger, J38

M.A. Thesis, J43
Martians, J44
Masque of Melancholy, J49
More Abundant Life, The, J11
Motlie Notis, J1
Mr. and Mrs. Jim Huttner, J32
Musical Propensities of VI Classical,
    On the, J2

Napoleon or Something, J21
New Boy Who Won Through, The,
    J2
Nineteen Questions for Social Blights,
    J33

Old Glory, Old Junk, J35

Paris in Chicago, J5
Pastoral for Maytime, J41

Question of the Beard, The, J48

Raw Lie Unraw, J31

Sir Lafournayse, The Passing of, J4
Society Notes, J2
Spring for All, J38
Spring gets Jester Editors, J18
Springtime for Webster, J13
Strasbourg Cathedral, J2
Students Awake, J11
Suburban Demon, J9
Success Story, J14

The Beetle Becomes the Prince, J52
They Grow in September, J24
Two Things for Christmas, J45

Unfortunate Oakhamian, An, J1

[113]

Juvenilia

Voyage to Nyack, J36

Wahlt Hitler, J3
What Goes On, J25

Window, J36
Woods are not Sober, J43

Your Night to Howl, J24, J29, J36

INDEX OF NAMES

Adams, J. Donald, B13
Addison, Agnes, C5
Agagianian, Gregory Peter XV Cardinal, A21
Agnes, St., G60
Anastacio, D. Timoteo Amoroso, D61
Augustine, St., B4

Baird, Sister Mary Julian, D69
Barbosa, D. Marcos, I21
Beilenson, Peter, A9
Berchmans, Mother M., A6, I14
Bernard, St., A19, B14, C42, C62, C66, C72, C74, C75, C79, D60, D70, E3, I6, I7
Binns, Harold, D25
Brunini, John Gilland, G47
Bruno, Eric, D36, D37
Burke, Bob, J16, J17

Carruth, Hayden, D18
Catherine, Saint, of Siena, I17
Catherine, Sister Mary, D31
Chautard, Jean-Baptiste, E2
Clement, St., A12, G40, G41
Comet, J., A18
Connolly, Francis X., D19
Crossman, R. H. S., C6
Cunningham, Sterns, D15

Davey, William, D59
De Budos, Madame Laurence, E1
De Lenval, Helene Lubienska, D43, D66
Dell'Isola, Frank, D68, D74
Delteil, Chanoine Francois, D35
De Osuna, Fray Francisco, C23
Der Heilige Johannes Vom Kreuz, C71
Dubbel, Earle S., D57

Egan, Joseph M., D47
Eliot, T. S., D69
Eudes, St. John, E1
Evans, Mary Ellen, D8

Fadiman, Clifton, B19, G59
Fairchild, Hoxie Neale, C9
Farrell, Walter, D50
Fremantle, Anne, B11

Gardiner, Harold C., D30, D58, D72
Gill, Barry, D9
Gillis, James M., D27
Giovanni, San, Della Croce, C70
Giustiniani, Paul, B21
Graham, Aelred, D51, D57, D59, D73
Gregory, T. S., D49
Guerric, Bl., C95

Herter, Christine, C4
Hughes, Richard, J50
Hunkeler, Leddegar, H38
Huttner, Jim, Mr. and Mrs., J32
Huxley, C12, J37
Hyde, Clara, C13

Irma, Sister Mary, D40

Jahan, E3
James, Bruno Scott, B14
Jerome, St., A5, G31
John, St., of the Cross, A16, B9, C42, C68, C69
John, St., the Baptist, A12, G33, G47
Jones, Gwyn, J45
Joselyn, Sister M., D39
Julie, Sister, D2

Keelan, B. C. L., B16
Kilmer, Joyce, G58
Kimball, Dudley, A2, A5
Knight, G. Wilson, C10
Koch, Rudolf, A9
Kothen, Robert, D65
Krikorian, Y. H., D26

Landy, Joseph, D53
Larraona, P. Arcadio, H52
Lauras, Antoine, D48
Lavaud, P. Benoit, H28
Lawrence, D. H., C11

[115]

Name Index

Lax, Robert, A5
Lelotte, F., D65
Lentfoehr, Sister M. Therese, C20,
C41, C46, C49, C52, D36, D37, D40,
D45, D46, D62, D67, D71
Lewis, C. S., C8
Lissner, Will, D10
Lowell, Robert, D1
Lowry, Robert, A2
Luce, Clare Boothe, B9
Lutgarde, St., A13

Madeleva, Sister M., D13, D50
Magaret, Helene, D16
Malachy, St., A12, D18, G41
Mansfield, Margery, D37
Marie, Francois De Ste., I20
McCauliff, George A., D3, D37
McSorley, Joseph, D32
Merton, John Paul, D46
Merton, Thomas, A1, A2, A3, A4, A5,
A6, A7, A8, A9, A10, A11, A12, A13,
A14, A15, A16, A17, A18, A19, A20,
A21, B8, B9, C13, C52, C54, C77,
D1, D3, D7, D11, D12, D18, D21,
D22, D23, D24, D28, D33, D34, D35,
D36, D37, D38, D39, D40, D42, D44,
D49, D50, D51, D53, D57, D59, D60,
D62, D63, D64, D65, D68, D69, D71,
D73, E1, E2, E3, F1, F2, F4, G39,
G49, G54, G55, H4, H31, I10, I13,
I17, I21, J51, J52
Mondrone, D., D41
Motte, George, F1

Nabokoff, Vladimir, C2
Nelson, William, C7
Nerber, John, D6
Nicholl, Louise T., D4
Nims, John Frederick, D5

O'Brien, John A., B5

Paul, St., I10, I11
Penido, D. Basilio, D63
Plato, C6
Politzer, Heinz, D34
Powys, John Cowper, C3
Pritchett, V. S., D25, D29

Quin, I. T., D44

Rago, Henry, D55
Ransom, John Crowe, C1
Raymond, M., B2
Redman, Ben Ray, D54
Rice, Edward, A5
Ringstrom, Algot, A1
Rodman, Selden, B1, G16
Rutledge, Denys, D64

Sauvageot, Yvonne (San Vageot), A9,
A11, A15, E3, F1
Scotus, Duns, A5, A12, G18, G45
Sheen, Fulton J., E1
Sheridan, F. X. (Thomas Merton),
J51, J52
Skelton, John, C7
Skillin, Edward S., B3, B20, G43
Sortais, M. Gabriel, H31
Stern, Karl, B7
Stone, Irving, B6
Speaight, Robert, F2, F3
Strahan, Speer, D7

Theall, Bernard, D56
Therese, St., of Lisieux, B9
Thielen, James A., D21
Thomas, Dylan, F2, G52
Thornton, Francis B., D12, G32
Tillyard, E. M. W., C8
Tindall, William York, C11
Tobin, James Edward, B8, G58
Tobin, T., D23
Toelle, Gervase, D24, D31, D33, D36,
D37, D38
Towne, Charles Hanson, G1

Undset, Sigrid, I17

Van Doren, Charles, B19, G59
Van Doren, Mark, G48, G50
Van Eyck, R., D25
Van Rensselaer, Mariana Griswold,
G1

Waugh, Evelyn, C33, D25, D29, F1
White, Helen C., G12
Wiess, Frank J., D11
Wilder, Amos N., G54
Woods, Ralph L., B12, B17, G46

Young, E. B., D60

[116]